# Restoring Canna's chapel

*This book is intended to be an easy read and is accompanied by around 120 photographs illustrating the whole story. It tells of living and working in the Highlands and the struggle to build and live on a remote Scottish island and the restoration of a beautiful old building. The book contains several chapters telling the story of the restoration of the Chapel; the problems of obtaining funding; the struggle with the weather; of how to deliver both men and material to the island; and the fight for survival.*

# Restoring Canna's chapel

ALASDAIR
ROSS
McKERLICH

First published in 2007 by
Alasdair Ross Mckerlich
Isaluinn
Badicaul
By Kyle of Lochalsh
Ross-shire
Scotland
IV40 8BB

ISBN  978-0-9557904-0-9


Designed and typeset by Jim Bruce and Tam Murray
Printed and bound by Midas Printing (HK) Limited

# Contents

The Author of this book would like to put on record his grateful thanks to his wife Annie, who assisted in the research of this book and for putting up with him, especially during the night when he would waken up and switch on the bedroom light to write down ideas that had come into his head. Thanks also to Julie Sinderberry for the cover design; to Lynne Kennedy, my next door neighbour for the setting out; to Peter Urpeth, and his anonymous assessor; and finally to the members of my wider family for their encouraging support.

# Index of photographs

# Prologue

I first saw Canna and St Edwards Chapel from the deck of a Princess 388 cabin cruiser one morning in June 1995. Little did I know on that blustery day how deep and personal my knowledge of the island and that building would become in the near future.

But why seven years later after one million pounds being spent, and a lot of blood, sweat and tears being shed, is this building still not being used and lived in?

One Friday lunchtime in late June of 1995 I received an unexpected telephone call from a friend — Alistair Macrae, a semi-retired bus company owner — asking if I fancied a trip to St Kilda that afternoon. It was a place I had wanted to visit for a long time and I jumped at his invitation, despite the fact it was issued at very short notice.

St Kilda is 56 miles west of North Uist and is the furthest westerly island of the Outer Hebrides. It is somewhere you would only think about going in a 36-foot cabin cruiser if you had been given a marine forecast showing at least three days of calm weather. The forecast was for a high pressure coming in, which would mean a settled spell of light northerly wind.

Later that afternoon, while Alistair organised the fuelling of the boat, Johnnie "Ach" Macrae and I went to the local grocery store to purchase the vitals — the food. We had a crew of four consisting of Alistair, his son David, myself and Johnnie who was, at the time, the local harbour master — sadly by the time of writing Johnnie had passed away.

We set off about 5.00pm in the hope of getting as far as North Uist that evening but unfortunately, as we went past the Kyle of Lochalsh lighthouse, we hit a stronger than expected northerly wind of around 25 miles per hour; if the weather was like this in the Inner Sound of Raasay, then although the cabin cruiser had the power and the capability, it would have made for a very uncomfortable crossing to the Western Isles and a virtually impossible landing when we finally reached St Kilda. Our intrepid voyage was to be a non-starter.

Admitting defeat, however, does not come easily to Highlanders, and with a full fuel tank and sufficient food to feed six people for at least a week (albeit there were only four of us on board for a three day journey), we quickly put our heads together and decided we would instead venture south, down through the Kylerhea narrows, and head for Tobermory. That would mean we would be sheltered from the worst of the wind and any we did experience would be on our stern.

The cabin cruiser — a Princess 388 — had a top speed of 24 knots and was more than capable of cruising through the Inner and Outer Hebrides in a gale, but if you are going away for a relaxing long weekend you do want to enjoy an element of comfort; there is no sense in going flat out on a 15 foot swell. By 8.30pm in the evening we were steaming through the Sound of Mull and had Tobermory in our sights.

At around 9.00pm we tied up alongside the pier and were ready for some light refreshment, so we made our way up to the Mishnish, a regular and somewhat infamous watering hole for thirsty sailors. As the evening progressed and the water of life began to flow more freely, someone came up with the splendid idea of going to Barra the next day as there was a festival on and, therefore, there would be plenty of craic (as our Irish neighbours would say).

The next morning we were up bright and early — well, Alistair was. Alistair is not a man who consumes the water of life but he does smoke a lot — so much so in fact, it is a wonder that when he had the Princess fitted out he did not include a chimney. To define "a lot" I mean about 60 fags a day — and with his fag he likes a cup of tea. His specification had included the installation of an electric cooker instead of a gas model because he was concerned that should there be a gas leak, it would get into the bilges and presumably, when he was lighting up one of his 60 daily cigarettes, he could have an explosion at sea.

Unfortunately for Alastair's guests, and anyone else within a half-mile radius, the electric cooker required the use of a noisy diesel generator every time he wanted a cup of tea and 6.30am on that Saturday morning was no different. He woke up, lit up, and started up the noisy generator, which meant we were all awake, whether we liked it or not! Fortunately we had tied up the night before on the Caledonian MacBrayne ferry berth and were far enough away from all the yachts tied up in Tobermory Bay that on this occasion it was only the crew of his cabin cruiser who got the unwanted early morning call.

Although we were awake it did not mean we had to get out of our beds — or so we thought. As I said, we had tied up on the Cal Mac berth and by now the Cal Mac ferry was on its way over from the mainland so it was all hands on deck to shift the Princess to a new spot. By then it was 7.00am and time for breakfast; a fry-up for all the crew would go down nicely after the previous evening's consumption. But young David was having none of it — he wanted cereal. Alas, cereal had not been on our Friday shopping list, but then Alistair remembered there was an old packet on board from an earlier voyage. Nine-month-old

Cornflakes, however, were not good enough and so David's breakfast was to be delayed for two hours until the shop opened.

While we sat around drinking tea and re-fuelling our bodies, Johnnie spent the time sorting out the charts on board and noticed that there was not a chart of Barra and the Castlebay harbour entrance. Unbeknown to the rest of us, Johnnie put this time to good use — he went to the shops in Tobermory to purchase some cornflakes for David, and while there bought a chart of Castlebay harbour.

As we watched David eat his new cereal a short while later, we discussed the possibility of now heading for Castlebay. There was one major problem with that idea said Alistair: "We don't have a chart of Castlebay harbour."

"Problem solved," said Johnnie, and produced the new chart, "so let's go!"

It was a beautiful day and as the festival would not liven up until late afternoon we thought we would take our time crossing the Minch — the expanse of sea between the mainland of Scotland and the Outer Hebrides. We arrived at Barra by mid-afternoon and tied up alongside the fishing boats. Not as good an idea as we thought though, for while it made for a far safer boarding and disembarking, every time a fishing boat returned with its catch it was also a prime flyover zone for the seagulls who seemed to enjoy annoying Alistair by using his boat as a target area for their "discharge".

After washing the Princess down twice over, we decided the lesser of the two evils was to cast off from the fishermen's pier and head for a courtesy mooring in the harbour, which meant we now had to use the Princess's rubber tender to get ashore.

The evening went well at the Castlebay dance but realising we had a somewhat dangerous form of transport to get us back to the Princess, we left the festivities around 11.00pm (well, most of us did!) and returned to the boat for bed.

Despite being woken up with Alistair and his early cuppa, we had a leisurely lie-in and another cooked breakfast before lifting anchor and heading home. Our route was to take us down through the Small Isles back to Skye and then Kyle. While we were passing Canna, the farthest out of the Small Isles, Alistair asked me if I had ever been, to which I replied "no".

"Would you like to go ashore?" he said.

As it was just approaching noon and Alistair knew the route in, we decided to go for a spot of lunch.

When you are entering Canna harbour by boat you can't see the pier until the last minute but what you can see — like a lighthouse guiding you in — is St Edwards Chapel, which was built by the Marquess of Bute at the turn of the century. This was my first sighting of it and little did I know then what lay ahead.

**St Edwards Chapel in 1995**

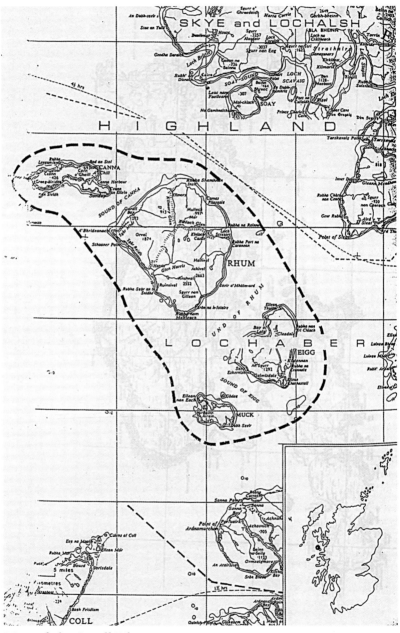

Map of the Small Isles

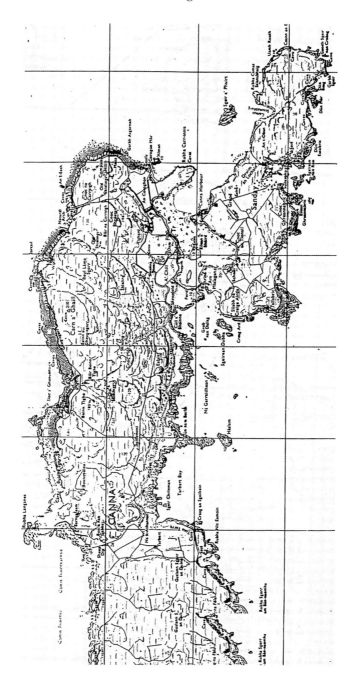

Map of Canna

CHAPTER ONE

# How the Chapel sucked in
# the author

I heard or saw no more of St Edwards Chapel until almost three years later in February 1998 when, as managing director of Donald Mckerlich & Son Ltd, I received a phone call from a firm of architects in Ayr asking if I would like to tender for the restoration project.

Donald Mckerlich & Son Ltd was set up in 1919 by my grandfather, Donald Mckerlich, who had served his time on the Clyde as a ship's joiner before he went off to fight for King and country during Word War I. After the war was over in 1918, he went back to his job on the Clyde but was very unsettled and so he came home to Kyle of Lochalsh, in the north-west Highlands of Scotland, to be nearer to his family. It was there he set up a small joinery repair firm.

My grandfather's firm soon grew in size and before long found themselves tendering to build complete new houses, which required several more tradesmen. In 1952, two years before I was born, my grandfather passed away and the firm went to my father, Alistair J R Mckerlich, who by now had been working for several years and served his time as a joiner with his father.

My father built up the firm to a workforce of 27 men who carried out some quite large contracts of up to six houses at a time, training several local tradesmen in joinery and masonry skills.

These loyal, skilled men were the backbone of the firm and it lived on its good name; Mckerlich's was fortunate to secure contracts in a 40-50 mile radius within Ross and Cromarty.

I was born in 1954 in Kyle and was educated at the local primary school and Plockton secondary school, before going to Lews Castle College at the age of 15 to study engineering. Unfortunately, although I secured an apprenticeship with BP, when I went down to London I failed the eye test and was told that owing to this I was no longer suitable for a marine engineering career with the company.

I returned home and started to work for my father who was a great believer that everybody had to start on the bottom rung of the ladder and climb their way up. And so, like my father, I served my time as a joiner in the family firm, being taught by the highly skilled tradesmen, some of whom had started working with my grandfather 30 years before.

In 1977 my father became very ill with cancer and died the day after his 53rd birthday and so it was on 1st June 1977, I was thrown in at the deep end, with only 6 weeks of office experience, and told to get on with it. I didn't like the paperwork then and my opinion never changed over the following years which brought an ever-increasing amount of it.

I enjoyed my time as a joiner and found it very rewarding; at the end of each day you could look back and see what you had achieved. In the office all you could see at the end of each day was a pile of paper. But I sadly realised that the paperwork was fundamental to the survival of the business and that was now down to me.

1977 was a very hard year with my mother dying a month after my father and my eldest brother committing suicide on the 16th August that same year. Fortunately I had, in 1974, married my wife Annie and by August 1977 we had two young children

— Trevor and Yvonne; they were my rock and my reason for carrying on. I put all my energy into rebuilding the firm and enjoying my family. I found keeping busy to be the best way forward, so with a young family and a firm of 17 employees being dependent on me to get the jobs in and pay their wages at the end of each week, there was plenty to do and a lot of late nights trawling through the never-ending heaps of paperwork.

Over the years, I trimmed the workforce a little to a more manageable size and, with the highly skilled tradesmen around me, we quickly secured the work to keep us all busy in and around the Lochalsh and south Skye area. As well as being involved in new house construction and major alterations to existing properties, we had also become involved in restoration works by way of securing a five-year winter contract to restore parts of Eilean Donan Castle at Dornie, which had been worn away by the ever-increasing summer visitors and the horrendous gales which pounded it every winter from the north, south, east and west.

Looking out of my office window on that late February afternoon in 1998, into gale-force winds and heavy rain showers, I had no hesitation in quickly thanking the architect's secretary for their invitation to restore St Edwards Chapel, but politely declined.

Some 14 days later the same architect (whom we had never worked with before) was back on the phone reminding me of all the work the firm had previously received from his client — the National Trust for Scotland. Would I not reconsider my interest in this job?

Whether it was a bout of madness or my being educated in a castle some 25 years before, or whether it was just the challenge, I'll never know, but I changed my mind and said that the firm would like to be considered.

Within seven days we were asked by the architect to forward him three client references and a list and total costs of contracts we had carried out over the last two to three years. He also wanted information on our insurance, our health and safety history and the trades that we carried in-house i.e. the number of men we employed and their various skills — joiners, bricklayers, stone masons, slaters, plasterers etc.

We were then informed that Donald Mckerlich & Son was to be included in a select list of contractors who would be invited to tender for the restoration of St Edwards Chapel and the rebuilding of Point House. We were also told that the budget for the contract was £650,000 and that a bill of quantities would be sent out in late June for pricing, with a four-week tender period.

What that meant was, the architect would send out a 3-400 page document itemising every nut and bolt required to carry out the contract, to four or five contractors and that these contractors were expected to spend up to 500 hours of unpaid time and make 40 to 50 unrefunded phone calls to enable them to complete and return their tender by a given fixed date. This would be in the full knowledge that if the job finally went ahead, only one contractor had any chance of recovering their costs and that if the job did not go ahead that only the architect and his in-house quantity surveyor would be paid .

During my time in the construction industry I have often wondered if this is fair. Building contractors are now the only people in this complicated equation who are expected to work for nothing. Both the architect and the quantity surveyor, with all expenses paid, are on a fixed percentage fee based on the total build costs whether or not the job goes ahead. Why are architects not on a fixed contract fee to carry out their work, the same as the builders? Maybe if the architects who drew the drawings for the Scottish Parliament were on a fixed fee they would not have let it go TEN times over budget!

By now it was obvious to me that although I knew of the

chapel, and had seen it from a distance, an island site visit was a must. I would also have to discuss my intentions with the workforce to gauge their response. Would they be prepared to spend a year travelling to a remote island to rebuild a 100-year-old chapel and demolish and rebuild a house? Obviously there were lots of questions to be asked and answered.

The boys' questions and answers I would leave until later as my mind, for now, was on a site visit. How do I get there? How long will it take? Will I get fed when I get there? Can I visit the site in a day? If not where can I stay? And most importantly, how do I get home? (Funnily enough all the questions I had just asked myself were to be the same questions to be asked by the boys.)

The first thing I did was to look at the Cal Mac timetable but that was of little help as I found that there was no day of the week, during the winter months, when I could get on and off the island in one day, far less give me sufficient time to look over the chapel and familiarise myself with the surrounding area. If only we had spent more time on Canna when we sailed there on the Princess in 1995! If only I had walked over to the chapel, then I would have had a better idea what I was up against.

After mulling over various options I finally decided to travel under my own steam, where I had total control; I would go on my inflatable — a 20-foot rubber dinghy with a rigid hull, which was fitted with two outboards — a 45hp Evinrude and a 50hp Yamaha which ran on 2-stroke petrol. The shortest route was to leave from Elgol on Skye, but I had no idea if there was a suitable slipway or firm enough beach to launch from. After making further local enquiries I was told that there was a good concrete slipway that we could leave from in all tidal conditions. Unfortunately, that was not entirely the truth, as we were soon to find out.

I decided that the trip would be far safer with two people, so

I asked my good friend Douglas if he would like to go with me. He jumped at the chance and as he was his own boss he could get off work at short notice when there was a suitable weather window.

Early one Saturday morning in May we drove to Elgol, towing the boat on a trailer over the Skye Bridge. When we arrived in Elgol the tide was low and, much to our horror, the far end of the jetty was not covered by the sea. Once again I found myself all geared up to go with favourable weather conditions but with a major obstacle in my way. There was no other alternative than to drive the trailer over the end of the jetty and hope that with a bit of brute force we could slide the boat, on the trailer rollers, into the sea.

Thankfully our plan worked and after successfully launching the boat, Douglas's 4x4 had the power to pull the empty trailer up over the jetty edge and above the high water mark. We carried out a final safety check on the boat and all our equipment, contacted Oban coastguard by radio to inform them of our intended passage and then we were off.

The crossing only took us about 40 minutes. When we arrived at Canna pier the first thing we had to do was to measure the depth of water alongside the pier at low tide (this was done by simply tying a weight onto the bottom of a measuring tape which we had taken with us and lowering it gently over the side of our boat in various positions along the length of the pier). We also measured the actual length of the pier face. This information would be critical in deciding the size of ship we could charter to take in all our equipment, should we get the job.

We had tied the boat securely to the pier and started walking along the gravel-track road to Canna House, when we noticed that part of the road had been washed away by the previous winter gales; what was left, in places, was an access road less than

6 feet wide. Not only that, but the overall width of the road was only 7 foot 10 inches wide which posed a problem as some of the plant that would be required for the job was 10 feet wide.

I then realised that St Edwards Chapel was not in fact on the Isle of Canna at all, it was on the Isle of Sanday. The two are joined by a narrow pedestrian bridge at high tide. To get across in a vehicle would only be possible when the tide was out, via a narrow firm route over a muddy sand bar (and I mean narrow — you could not afford to deviate off this tried and tested track, which I can only assume had been used since tractors were brought onto Canna).

On walking past Canna House and on to Canna Farmhouse, we found the road went through a courtyard, set between the farmhouse and the outbuildings which again was far too narrow for our wide plant. It became clear that as well as repairing the main road, we would have to form a ramp off the road in front of the farmhouse and onto the shore, permitting us to drive our plant round the farmhouse and its buildings, before crossing the sand bar.

**Our rigid inflatable on the shore below Point house with Canna Harbour in the background**

Canna pier

The gravel access road to Canna House

The firm track over the sand bar at low tide

The pedestrian bridge connecting Sanday to Canna photographed from Canna...

...and from Sanday

The track on Sanday shore

Point House with Compass Hill directly behind and Canna Prison Hill over to the right

When we reached the pedestrian bridge to Sanday, Douglas and I split up. He went back for the inflatable and I carried on over the footpath which led to St Edwards Chapel. We arranged to meet up again on the beach below Point House. I was also keen to identify a route along the shore edge which we could use as an access track to bring our plant and equipment up to the chapel.

At Point House, I found all that remained were ruins fit for demolition. A complete rebuild would be required, so I didn't waste much time looking over it. Instead I walked up to the very imposing chapel, which was perched on the top of a small hill with nothing around it. What a strange place to build anything, far less a place of worship, I thought; the nearest houses or ruins were half a mile away. Who was the chapel built for and where were the people expected to come from to worship in this once magnificent building?

On close inspection I found the main outer shell of the chapel virtually intact, except for the front entrance porch which had had its roof re-felted although it required re-slating. There was also a very disconcerting crack running the entire length of the bell tower on its south west elevation. The front door was intact, as were most of the stained-glass windows, but there was no back door. You could see that with no back gate and part of the perimeter wall fallen down, cows and sheep were the only current users of the chapel these days.

All the timber floors were rotten as was the first floor in the bell tower. There were slight signs of dampness on the internal walls and a piece of plaster was missing from the apse wall (this piece of missing plaster held a lot of information had it been analysed and researched fully). Also missing was a length of the lightning conductor strap on the bell tower.

I had seen enough of St Edwards Chapel and Point House, and it was now time to return home. Much to our surprise we had

Various elevations of St Edwards Chapel as seen in 1998

The crack on the outside and inside of the bell tower

Two elevations (above and below) of Point House

**The missing plaster on the apse wall**

not glimpsed any of the inhabitants of either Sanday or Canna, the only people we met were a couple of tourists walking along the road. But, as is the case in small townships all over the Highlands, nothing goes unnoticed! I was informed at a pre-site meeting in Ayr 18 months later, at the architect's office, that the locals were well aware of our visit and they knew all about it, from the minute we arrived until the moment we left.

After the pre-departure checking of equipment and fuel, we set off back to Elgol. On our way home we spotted a basking shark and slowed down to take a look. Giving it a wide berth, we carried on our way but to our horror, some two minutes later, the 45hp engine cut out. You have never seen two people scan the ocean so fast to see if the shark was still around, it was like a scene from Jaws. Fortunately the engine had only run out of fuel and as we had plenty spare on board we quickly topped up the tank and were on our way again. We arrived safely in Elgol, and got the boat back on the trailer with no difficulty as the tide was now well in over the jetty.

CHAPTER TWO

# Final funding obtained by an Act of God

The 300 page bill of quantities and 20-30 tender drawings arrived by post in my office a couple of months later on 10th of July 1998, giving us a return date of the 7th of August. The work comprised the repair and alteration of St Edwards Chapel, including repairs to the tower, a study centre and ancillary accommodation. This included reroofing, external stonework repairs, new interior structure, floors, partitions, finishes and services, construction of a small generator house, access road, associated external works, drainage and external services systems.

The layout consisted of a front entrance porch leading into a hallway, with a disabled toilet to the left, and a dining area to the right with a sitting room off, a utility room, boiler room and a kitchen housed in the bell tower ground floor.

The first floor was made up of three work stations, one of which, by way of a viewing gallery, looked down to the dining and sitting area. The second floor had five bedrooms and two toilets and shower blocks, all tucked within the vaulted roof space. All floors were accessed by way of a self-supporting concrete fireproof stair.

When this work was completed, it was intended to use St Edwards Chapel as a study centre and accommodation unit for students to come, live on Sanday and study the Gaelic collection of the late John Lorne Campbell, which is presently housed in Canna House.

Knowing that we were on the tender list, I had, on my return from the site visit, started to contact the sub-contractors Mckerlich's usually employed to carry out electrical, plumbing, painting, heating and slating work. The responses were mixed; some owing to the remote location were simply not interested while others were only lukewarm. It was much the same from my own workforce — some of the men simply said: "No way" and others, it was clear, were going to need a lot of persuading.

Accommodation on the island was also going to be problematical. I contacted the four landladies on Canna but only received one positive response. Transportation for the men on a weekly basis and for the plant and material also had to be thought about.

PDG had a helicopter based in Kyle which was only used first thing in the morning and last thing in the late afternoon, so as I had promised the workmen that I would look at every option, I got in contact with PDG's base at Dalcross airport in Inverness, asking for a quote to fly eight people from Kyle on a Monday morning and flying them home on a Saturday afternoon — for 52 weeks. I knew it was an expensive mode of travel but even I got a shock when the quote arrived — £85,000! Although it was by far the quickest option, taking just 23 minutes each way, that mode of transport was very quickly knocked on the head. Purchasing our own boat and skipper was another idea but again that worked out not to be cost effective — or so we thought at that time.

After a hectic time pricing every item and making innumerable phone calls and I don't know how many faxes and letters, I started to add up all the figures and much to my horror, even after trimming them several times, the total quote came to over £1 million. How on earth could I have got it so wrong? We had never tackled a contract of such a high value. I re-checked my sums over and over again but I couldn't cut costs any further, so I posted my tender by recorded delivery in time for it to reach the architect's office by the given return date, feeling very deflated; the whole exercise had been a thorough waste of time.

Very much to my surprise, we heard back from the architect informing us that our tender was the cheapest received, but that our quote was 60 per cent over budget and savings would have to be found if this job was to go ahead. (Are some architects woefully optimistic at the expense of others? Or are they so far away from reality that, although our quote was the cheapest of five received — and, I have since been reliably informed, nearly half of the highest tender received — it was still £400,000 over budget. Architects still advise their clients to proceed with the drawings and planning application knowing full well that the project has no hope of coming within budget. Or is it that they know that if they start the drawings they will not have wasted any of their time and they still get paid so to hell with everyone else.

Despite the fact that I had already spent weeks of my time on this project, I now found myself being asked, along with others involved, to look for savings. This period of possible cost cutting lasted weeks and even with the rebuilding of Point House removed from the contract (which affected our accommodation plans as it had been our intention to concentrate on the rebuild of this and then move in to save on our accommodation costs), and with the removal of all the buildings around St Edwards Chapel, we still could not get our quote in line with the client's budget.

At the end of these protracted negotiations the project was once again put on hold until 1999. In the winter of 1998-1999, the chapel was hit by lightning on the cross which stood on top of the bell tower, which set the roof of the bell tower on fire. The fire smouldered for three of four days before the bell tower fell in (it was only then that the fire was detected by the islanders). The fire also damaged the bell tower and brick arches and the heat cracked the ornamental sandstone lintels.

As the chapel had been insured we then found ourselves splitting up our quote yet again and forming a separate quote to cover the fire damage to the bell tower roof. Adding the insurance company payment for the bell tower to the client's budget, there was sufficient money to award the contract to Donald Mckerlich & Son Ltd to the value of £650,000. We had 12 months to complete the contract. We were also expected to be on site within 28 days.

**The fire damaged bell tower roof**

CHAPTER THREE

# Preparation required to
# carry out contract

Canna is part of a group of islands in the Inner Hebrides, known as the Small Isles, which also includes Rum, Eigg and Muck. They form a complete group of contrasting islands within the wider coastal setting of the Cuillin on Skye, Morar, Moidart and Ardnamurchan.

Each island has a different landscape, character and outline and the sea inevitably plays an important role in setting off and linking the varying shapes of the islands, which make a major contribution to a seaboard of the highest scenic quality.

Canna lies about three miles north-west of Rum and also consists of the smaller island of Sanday which is connected to Canna at low tide. The coastline of Canna is made up mainly of steep cliffs capped by a ridge of wet heath and blanket bog. Sanday and the more low-lying areas of Canna support a varied range of coastal grassland and heath communities. They are of particular importance for their sea bird colonies and birds of prey. The large breeding population of Shags is of national significance and there are important populations of other sea birds including Manx Shearwater, Puffin, Fulmar, Razorbill, Black Guillemot, and on the low-lying ground you will find the Corncrake. Much to the islanders' delight, they had also recently spotted two pairs of Sea Eagles nesting on the island.

Canna was once part of the endowment of the famous monastery on Iona, founded by St Columba in the sixth century. After the reformation, a thousand years later, it became part of the possessions of Clanranald, a branch of the great Macdonald Clan. Clanranald also owned several other islands in the Hebrides and estates on the neighbouring mainland, where their chief lived in Castle Tioram in Moidart.

Canna had five owners in its long history — the Church; the Clanranald-Macdonalds, until they sold it to a merchant, MacNeill from Campbeltown in 1835, who sold it again in 1881 to Robert Thom, a man who had adequate capital behind him to make considerable improvements. He and his family had made their money in importing hardwood timber. His knowledge of hardwood he put to good use when selecting the timber to be used on Canna pier

He also had a great knowledge of farming and built up a fine herd of pedigree Highland cattle, which he knew would thrive on the lush Canna pastures. The improvements he made also included the construction of a green heart pier, which encouraged the Barra herring fishermen to come in and land their catch and subsequently led to a curing station being built. The Sanday crofters also had help to improve their houses.

Robert Thom died in 1911, and was commemorated by the erection of a Presbyterian Church on Rubha Cairinnis, a copy of an early Irish church building in Glendalough.

It was from Robert Thom's grandson that John Campbell bought Canna in 1938.

Thom gifted a site on Sanday to the Marquesss of Bute, as the original Roman Catholic chapel was a small building on Canna near the former graveyard at Keill.

The chapel on Sanday was built by Lady Bute in memory of her father, Edward, Lord Howard of Glossop, and was completed in 1890, dedicated to St Edward the Confessor. The architect was William Frame and the face carvings were by Thomas Nicholls. Two of the face carvings were set in the corner of the Chapel, and were of senior gentlemen who were supporting large moustaches; there was a further two of slightly younger men with moustaches and beards; a further two were of middle-aged ladies and the remaining four were of younger ladies. There was a much larger community on Sanday then and the harbour was being well used by fishermen from Barra and Eriskay, who were all Catholics.

Canna, and I can only assume Sanday, were gifted to the National Trust for Scotland in 1981 by the late John Lorne Campbell, a writer and historian who spent many years in the Outer Hebrides, especially the Uists, researching the Gaelic language. He died 15 years later in 1996. His gift also included virtually all the property there so St Edwards Chapel was part of that gift.

With St Edwards belonging to the NTS how were we now finding ourselves signing a contract to carry out a full restoration on this building with the Hebridean Trust? Well, we were informed that the NTS had sold St Edwards and the surrounding ground to the Hebridean Trust for a nominal fee. This enabled the Hebridean Trust to apply to all the funding bodies for grant assistance, with the main money coming from the Lottery Fund.

After the major cost cutting exercise had taken place, the option of staying the full length of the contract with the landladies had gone. So also had the quick mode of travel to the island by helicopter, with travelling times suiting our own timetable. The whole exercise had meant a complete rethink on how we were going to run this contract. What we finally decided on, and what was within the budget, was to ship out our two portable-cabin

The 10 face carvings in St Edwards Chapel

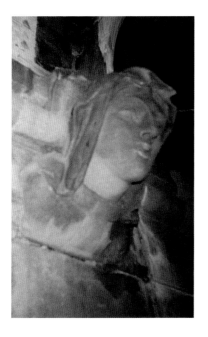
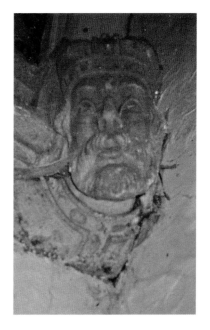

offices with an additional five and connect them together as one unit to form a complete office and accommodation complex. This was the most economical option in terms of heating and lighting. With that decision now taken, we obviously required a considerably bigger ship with a lot of deck space on which to transport everything. It would also need to be fitted with a large crane for offloading. More importantly, we would need a very large generator and plenty of fuel to run it for that was to be our life line.

St Edwards Chapel was not like any site that we had previously worked on — the only facility available to us was water; no road, no power, no telephone and no shop or builders' merchant to go to if we had forgotten anything. (Actually I tell a lie, there was a shop but it only opened in the summer and only when the Cal Mac ferry came in and all it sold was visitor trinkets

Canna shop with island generator fuel storage tank on the right

**Canna Prison**

and maps — no milk, bread, pies, juice or daily papers, which up until now seemed to be the staple diet of the building trade.)

We looked at various boats, landing craft and ships that had a large enough deck space, sufficient tonnage, shallow draught and were still short enough to tie up alongside Canna pier. We also tried to obtain a quote from Cal Mac. While they were happy to assist where possible, owing to their tight summer schedule, they were unable to release a ship at the short notice we now required, given the very tight on-site start date. We soon found that the other shipping companies were no different — you could not charter a ship within a week or so like you could hire a piece of plant in the construction industry.

In the end, we decided to charter the *Highland Carrier* — a 1000-ton cargo ship with a fairly shallow draught, which also had a 40-ton deck crane. The ship was working out of Kyle of Lochalsh, transporting mostly perishable cargo on a daily basis to Stornoway on the Isle of Lewis but was available for charter at the weekend.

The time had come to work out the first load. By now it was clear that a large cost in this contract would be the double handling of material or, in this case, the nine-fold handling. What I mean by that is having to manhandle the same item of building material over and over again; these days men's labour time is very expensive and you try to minimise the amount of time spent when workmen (either by hand or by machine) load or unload the same item of building material before it is fixed on site. We were faced with the material being loaded onto our suppliers' transport in Inverness, Glasgow or wherever (1), unloading that same item in our yard in Kyle for storage (2), being reloaded onto a truck to be delivered to the harbour (3), unloading it onto the jetty (4), loading it onto the *Highland Carrier* (5), unloading it off the ship when it arrived at Canna (6), loading it onto our tractor and trailer

*Highland Carrier*

on Canna pier (7), for its onward journey along the road track and across the sand bank to Sanday at low tide across the Sanday shore track and up our new road to St Edwards Chapel, offload at the site (8), and finally fix in position (9) in St Edwards Chapel.

We spent three weeks getting our first boat load together. All in all we bagged 250 tonnes of Type 2 road material, 100 tonnes of building sand, concrete mix, pipe gravel and gravel chips in 1 ton bags for easier onward transportation. We crated 20 tonnes of slates, securely tie-banded timber, cement, roof joists, sarking, reinforcing rods, 30 tonnes of scaffolding, security fencing panels etc. With all our other material and plant requirements we now had a total ship load of just less than 500 tonnes, not to mention the 30 barrels each carrying 45 gallons of diesel and the two 45-gallon drums of petrol. Also included in our first load were the gabion baskets which we filled in Kyle to make them easier to handle and save time and the material we required to repair the road up to Canna Farm.

Our charter agreement allowed us five hours to load, four hours steaming time to get to Canna, four hours to unload and four hours to return to Kyle, before the *Highland Carrier* was back on her normal run to Stornoway. As she did not return from Stornoway until 12 noon each day, and we were not allowed to bring our cargo onto the pier until Saturday morning, it was, as you could imagine, a hectic day with all hands on deck.

The skipper of the *Highland Carrier* was from Liverpool and as he was not familiar with the Inner Hebrides, far less the Small Isles, he wanted to arrive in Canna in daylight, so he is in total control of his ship and the ship's cargo. We left Kyle at 2.00am following a well earned rest after completing loading at 6.00pm.

When we were approaching Canna, the skipper of the *Highland Carrier* asked me up to the bridge because the compass

The various items of cargo and portable cabins being crated and loaded at Kyle pier

had gone wonky, and he could not actually see any pier that was remotely capable of tying his ship against.

Canna has a 139m high hill (Compass Hill), close to the pier which is formed of volcanic rock known as *tuff* of such a high iron content that nearby ships' compasses are distorted, pointing East rather than North.

Tuff is a type of rock consisting of consolidated volcanic ash ejected from vents during a volcanic eruption.

Canna pier is tucked round a rock face and is not visible until the very last minute and there is a nasty rock at its top end that is visible at low tide. As you can imagine the skipper was rightly being very cautious as he knew he would have to turn his ship round and drop his anchor to pull himself off the pier on his departure.

We arrived in Canna at 8.30am and Packie (with whom we had been in regular contact) met us at the pier, took our ropes and assisted us in tying up the *Highland Carrier*. As she did not have an MCA certificate for more than 12 passengers we were restricted to only taking seven workmen, including myself and my son Trevor, who was home on holiday and was keen to see what on earth his father had taken on.

CHAPTER FOUR
# Problems restoring on such a remote location

It took us four hours working flat out to unload the *Highland Carrier* and all her curtain side containers. We moved all we could away from the face of the pier for safety reasons and left eight feet of clear walking space as the Cal Mac ferry was expected in the next morning.

After the unloading was done, we made our way up to the vacant shepherd's cottage which we had rented from Packie's wife Wendy for our first two working trips, by which time our own camp would, hopefully, be up and running. We had also arranged with Wendy that our rental agreement allowed for her cooking our evening meal but that we would make our own breakfast and lunch.

It was now the end of June and the longest day was behind us which meant it was a race against time to get St Edwards wind and watertight before the winter weather set in. However, nothing could be done until the road to Canna Farm was repaired. We had already identified the damaged areas of road and Johnnie, our machine operator, started to excavate the damaged areas down to the hard rock base while we set about lifting in the pre-filled gabion baskets (these are used as a method to contain large rocks in an area when you do not have a solid face to build from, and

The *Highland Carrier* alongside Canna pier

All our material and equipment being unloaded onto Canna pier

consist of a square cube of strong reinforced netting, with a top hinged door, to enable you to place the rock fill into the cube) to form a firm edge. Using bags of road material we had brought with us, we then did some in filling. There were also several large pot-holes in the road so the whole job took us a couple of days.

As our portable cabins were too wide to squeeze between the farm house and the outbuildings we had to form a ramp off the road and onto the beach. In fact, having done a site visit, I had already known there was a major problem: our portable cabins were 30 feet long and 10 feet wide and the road was only seven feet 10 inches wide, with a natural stone wall running tight alongside the full length of the road from Canna House to the farm, which would prevent us turning tightly round any corner.

Back in Kyle of Lochalsh, before we left, we had made a trailer for this very problem. The first unit, the welfare shower and toilet block, which was twice as heavy as any of the other units, was lifted on using a forklift at each end. It was then secured onto the self-steer trailer which in turn was towed by a 75hp, 4-wheel-drive tractor. After checking everything, and with a man on each corner of each unit, we started on our two-mile journey at slow pace, with the 4-wheeled rough-terrain telescopic forklift travelling directly behind.

The first three-quarters of a mile to the farm took us two hours; the trip required several stops so that the teleforklift could lift the unit round the corners and we then had to wait for the tide to go out and expose the sand bar to Sanday Island.

Tides run on a 14-day cycle with very high tides and very low tides one week, followed by seven days of small tides, during which the sand bar would not be exposed. Each tide, from high to low, takes six hours and 15 minutes to flow and the same time to ebb. As the whole process happens twice in a 25-hour period, the time of the low tide is advanced by sixty minutes each day.

The storm damage to the retaining walls of the road up to Canna Farm

The gabion baskets retaining the road edge

An hour later the tide was low enough for us to continue our journey across the sand bank onto Sanday Island. This turned out to be the easiest part of the journey; once we got over the exposed sand bar, we had to follow a very rough track at the top of the shore. Halfway along the track disaster struck and the steering mechanism collapsed on the trailer so the rest of the day was spent trying to repair it.

The next day, repairs complete, we made our way through the gate and up through the field, along the existing hard track to St Edwards Chapel where we finally offloaded the welfare unit at the top end of our site. It took two very hard days to get it on site and we still had another six units to go. As I walked, exhausted, back to the cottage for dinner, I looked down to the harbour at the £250,000 of equipment and thought to myself: "What on earth am I doing here and what on earth have I let myself in for?" The only thing in our favor that fateful day was that we managed to get the tractor back across the sand bar and onto Canna on the second low tide in the evening.

One problem remained, however. As the original trailer was now a complete write-off, how were we going to get the remaining six portable cabins across? We finally decided to use the only other large trailer we had with us (although far from ideal owing to its shorter wheel base, it was all we had), but which first had to have its load of security fencing panels removed.

The next day as we waited for the tide to go out, we started to prepare the second set of units for their journey. As soon as the sand bar was sufficiently exposed, we drove the tractor and trailer onto Sanday and up to the site, closely followed by the telehandler which we needed to unload the fencing from the trailer.

When our tractor and trailer got back to the pier we quickly loaded the second portable cabin, sitting it on top of several timber sleepers, which would enable us to lift the unit above the height of the stone wall allowing our 12-foot overhanging unit to turn round the tight corners.

Again we set off at a slow pace with a man keeping watch on each corner of the portable cabins in the event that part of it might catch the stone wall, the telehandler following slowly behind us.

Fortunately when we got to the farm with the second unit the sand bar was still exposed, which enabled us to cross over and on up to our site. It had been a better day as we had managed to complete the task in just one day.

In the early hours of the next morning, working around the tides, three of us went back over to Sanday to bring the tractor and trailer back to Canna, albeit by torchlight, for reloading at 8.00am.

What we could have done without was the early morning phone call from the architect, telling us that we had deviated off the agreed route by going through the best hay field on the island. Ironically, the whole time we were on Sanday, through two harvest seasons, we never saw anyone either planting or cutting hay on this field. "What on earth was going on," I thought. We were now being told to stop using the safest access, and instead use a far more dangerous, slippery route. I couldn't help seeing the irony in the situation when, just the month before at the pre-start meeting in Ayr, we were handed a safety document for the complete works — The Health and Safety Plan — which emphasised the "safe way of working".

During his call, the architect had also asked us why we were working through the night as there had been no mention of this at the pre-site meeting.

Phone calls like these continued on a daily basis and after two weeks the reports about our work had become greatly exaggerated — not to mention extremely annoying — because each time the architect telephoned the site office, someone working in the chapel had to down tools and run to answer the telephone, only to find the architect had been given another incorrect report on our works. We had to find who was sending these reports and, more importantly, why?

One person's name immediately sprang to mind; this person had already been asked and had denied all knowledge of calls to the architect. There was nothing for it but to set an old builder's trap; we told three different stories to three different people who were all possible suspects, but kept the juiciest story for our real suspect, whom we told that, on lifting the timber floor in the chapel we had found what looked like two gold coins.

True to form, the very next morning the architect was on the phone reminding us of the contract conditions, "anything of value found on or near the chapel had to be immediately handed over". The trap had worked and we had our man. All the workmen were told not to discuss anything happening on the site with this person in the future.

Individuals who behave in this way, telling outrageous untruths, and then when questioned deny any involvement, can only be described as a "kipper"; a herring that has been split in half, gutted, had its backbone removed, and filleted, thereby making it two-faced, spineless and gutless!

While we appreciated that with us coming onto this sparsely-populated island and virtually doubling the population overnight would mean we were bound to be the main attraction, and although we were very grateful that people were concerned about our safety, especially during the night, we could have done without someone telling tales to the architect of our every move.

In an ideal situation we would have had six weeks to excavate our proposed access road, backfilling and compacting it with our road material and then using it to get our units on site. However,

The route we were forced to use to get our offices onto the site

we were faced with a far from ideal situation; a race against tide and time in getting the chapel re-roofed before the winter gales set in. Now that the second unit was on site we were ready to load the next one but were delayed because we had to wait for the island's lifeline ferry to arrive.

This concerned me greatly; we were not working in a safe environment when the Cal Mac ferry and its passengers were alongside the jetty. Like all island communities, while it was not unusual to go all day without seeing anyone, when the ferry came in the island came alive, and every man and his dog came down to catch up on all the gossip (which, of course, we were now part of).

After the ferry left we carried on with our loading — time and tide wait for no man. As each unit was transferred, so we became more efficient at the job and, with us working through the night, we had all the cabins on site by the end of our first trip, even managing to take the last two units over in one day. It was now time to return home to Kyle to recharge our batteries. My son Trevor had to leave halfway through the trip as he had to return to college in Glasgow. His journey off the island involved him taking the Small Isles ferry back to Mallaig. With no onward ferry connection to Armadale in Skye at that time of year, he then had to take the train to Fort William where he was met by his mother, Annie, who had driven down from Kyle to pick him up. This was a journey the rest of us would become very familiar with over the months that followed.

Owing to our cost cutting exercise we had decided that our mode of transport on and off Canna was to be the Cal Mac ferry to Armadale on Skye then by minibus up through south Skye, and over the toll bridge to Kyle.

On our second trip out to Canna, my wife Annie joined us to assist in fitting out the kitchen and dining area of our (soon to be) new accommodation. She was going to hang up curtains, scrub out the units, and generally giving a homely feel to the whole place.

Meanwhile, our first job was to level the portable cabins and bolt them together to make one large 70-foot-long unit. Colin, our electrician, wired all the units together and connected them to our 60kva generator, while everyone else mucked in tying the units down and constructing a skirt between them and the ground to prevent the winter gales from getting underneath and blowing them away. While we were doing that, Johnnie, the machine operator, concentrated on getting some of the 45-gallon drums of fuel over from Canna to fire up the generator; he also installed a temporary septic tank for the waste.

By the end of our second trip we had done everything we had to in order for us to move in at the start of our next trip. Everything, that is, but for a 10 pence olive that had been removed from a half-inch plumbing fitting. Much to our chagrin this olive was going to take up to five days to complete its mammoth journey. Our office in Kyle would post it, and would travel 83 miles east to the Inverness sorting office, then all the way back to the west coast to Mallaig, where it would be sorted into the Small Isles post, from where it would then have to wait for the next available ferry to Canna. During the winter the ferry ran just three times a week; it would have been quicker to send it from Kyle to New Zealand!

As we had now decided to cater for ourselves we were in need of a cook; one who had the skill to keep up to 17 men satisfied three times a day and could also handle the isolation. My sister Anne happened to be looking for a job and although she had not catered for quite such a large group for a few years, she certainly had the requisite skills. She had been taught in Duncraig Castle College near Plockton which was renowned in the catering world. While the men were not expecting cordon bleu catering and silver service, we did intend to provide them with good wholesome food.

It is said that the way to a man's heart is through his stomach.

Our theory being: a contented workforce would be a productive workforce

The catering was a combined effort between my wife Annie and my sister. Although Annie had not been taught at Duncraig, she had spent four years cooking in Stromeferry Hotel before we were married and, more importantly, she was very experienced in ordering food for bus loads of people.

The reason this was an issue is that Canna has no shop far less a supermarket, where we could purchase the amount of food required for each trip. So, not for the first time Annie came to the rescue and took on the task of travelling through to Inverness every fortnight, purchasing the food, bringing it back to Kyle and packing it into commercial cool boxes for its onward journey to Canna.

Owing to the lengthy travelling times to and from the island, I had agreed with the boys that we would work for 10 days then take four days off, arranging our trips around the Cal Mac timetable. This meant we required food for 17 men for 10 days at a time. All this food had to be carried onto the boat in Armadale, off the boat in Mallaig, onto the Small Isles ferry, off the ferry when we arrived at Canna, into our trusty petrol Landover up to the farm, then carried by hand over the pedestrian bridge and onto the tractor and trailer which would take it up to the accommodation block which the architect was to christen "the Horizontal Hilton" on his first site visit.

After returning to site for our first full 10 day working trip, and with our new cook on board, our first task was to start up the generator which in turn switched all the power on in the Horizontal Hilton, which would power our freezer and fridges.

The Horizontal Hilton next to St Edwards Chapel

Two of the younger members of the team would assist Anne in unpacking all the food provisions.

Had it not been for my wife Annie, who had remained in Kyle, we might not have eaten that first night. She had thought of everything and knowing that the ferry would not get us into Canna until mid-afternoon, and that by the time we finally got the food to camp it would be pretty late for Anne the cook to prepare a full evening meal, Annie had been busy at home the previous evening putting together our first camp dinner. All we had to do when we finally got to Canna was to prepare the veg and cook the tatties, which was our new cook's first task.

Our first task, meanwhile, was to make the site secure which we did by carefully lifting the heavy security fence panels around the site and slotting them into concrete blocks. We needed a lot of panels because we had to fence off the chapel, which was itself enclosed by a stone wall, and all the way back up to the Horizontal Hilton to prevent anybody from getting in to our working area.

We had not expected to receive any unannounced visitors. However, we hadn't considered the regular visiting yachts which used the natural sheltered harbor. They would sail in, drop anchor and row ashore in their small rubber tenders to the bay below Point House, as they had done on previous trips, and then walk up to St Edwards Chapel fully expecting to get inside.

These yacht crews were now, of course, not particularly pleased to be informed that St Edwards was currently a construction site and they were not permitted access for the duration of the works. "But this chapel has been open for years and is a lovely place to visit!" they would dispute.

Once the site was secure we had to erect scaffolding around the whole chapel, including the bell tower. As a result of the earlier lighting strike and subsequent fire, this task had to be done

Some of the visiting vessels in Canna's natural harbour

Some of the visiting vessels in Canna's natural harbour

with extreme care because of the possibility of falling masonry. It was essential that the workmen wore personal protective equipment (PPE) at all times, including a safety hat.

To scaffold a building of this height it would be normal practice to drill tying eyes into the existing masonry wall, but because St Edwards was a listed building and constructed from facing stone, on this occasion we were not allowed to follow that procedure.

As we were scaffolding three sides of the bell tower at a time this gave us two solid corners and, with the aid of a few back stays, the scaffold was rigid enough until we got up to the first of the bell tower arches. There we set about constructing the scaffolding building clamp which had been engineered to overcome the lack of building anchors.

What the clamping job consisted of was passing four scaffold tubes around the tower base of the bell arch, clamping the tubes tight to the building, then feeding four more scaffold tubes through the bottom of the tower arches until they came out of the opposite side of the tower and clamping them onto the perimeter tubes. This procedure was repeated at the top of the arch. We then placed two vertical timber battens on each of the four corners and drove hardwood timber wedges between the scaffold clamp and the timber battens. This was repeated on the next level, not only giving us a secure point for our box scaffold to be fixed onto, but also clamping and stabilising the entire tower and preventing it from bowing out when it came to dismantling the remainder of the burnt bell tower roof timbers.

When we finally got up to the top of the bell tower we saw the cross precariously wedged on two burnt rafters and leaning onto the stone gable wall. How it had remained there and how we were going to get it safely back down to the ground, I did not know.

The bell tower scaffolding clamp

The scaffolding around the bell tower

The scaffolding around the bell tower

The scaffolding around the bell tower

We also came across a date and initials on one of the sandstone sills of the bell tower arches (GML July 1889) presumably belonging to one of the stone masons working on the original construction of the Chapel.

The original inner bell tower roof was covered in six inches of bird droppings and until these faeces were removed we could not ascertain the condition of the inner roof.

Our attention turned to the inside of the bell tower, where we now started to erect a scaffold tower to support the underside of the tower floor. On our way up we came across the actual bell itself. The only reason it was still here was because of its difficult, inaccessible location which had stopped the treasure hunters from removing it.

The task now was to carefully remove the bell, which had its top hinge broken, and carefully crate it up for its final onward journey to the new chapel which was to be built on the converted blacksmiths shed alongside Canna Farm.

Once we got the bell safely stored we were able to proceed with our inner scaffold support, and then kit up with disposable boiler suits, gloves and face masks in order to remove the bird poo. We shovelled up 40 bags of starling droppings before we reached the beautiful lead roof, which unfortunately had to come out because the intention was for the new cold water storage tanks to sit on that floor and in order for that to happen, steel beams had to be inserted to take the extra weight.

Water had always been a problem on the island because Canna had limited reservoir capacity and the pressure was not very good, particularly in high up sites like the one we were working on. Three cold water tanks, each with a storage capacity of two hundred gallons, were to be installed and the water required to fill them would be pumped up at night when there was little or no demand from the island's residents.

The cross sitting on the gable

The Chapel bell

Date and initials found on the sandstone sill

**Starlings roosting on our scaffolding**

But we had a problem. The starlings were not for giving up their home without a fight; night after night they returned, even if we were still working. They would fly in through the bell tower fins giving us as much of a fright as they themselves got when they happened upon us.

The starlings were persistent. But at least the workmen could not say that they never had any birds visit them while working on Canna, albeit 99 per cent of them were of the feathered variety!

Although it was intended to fit lids and insulate the cold water storage tanks, it was extremely important that we stopped the birds from getting into the bell tower because with them could come infection. Although people should drink the water from taps that are connected to the rising main (which is normally the kitchen tap), and not from any tap that is fed from a storage tank, they often do brush their teeth using a tap in the bathroom and take a glass of water to bed.

We found the starlings were even able to squeeze through the new timber bell fins. The only way we finally stopped them was by fitting removable zinc fly screen panels to all the new bell tower arches.

After we had supported the underside of the lead floor we erected a further scaffold on top of the tower to gain access to the cross. By constructing an overhead gantry, and with the use of a block and tackle, we tied the cross to this rope apparatus. Neil, our foreman joiner, was given the onerous task of cutting the cross free and finally, after much preparatory work, we lowered the cross to the ground.

Neil, who was from the Isle of Barra, had no problem coping with the remoteness of living and working in Canna, but what he did miss was his practising every second Thursday with the local Gaelic choir. Neil was a member of Strath Gaelic Choir, and a fluent Gaelic speaker. He had recorded the songs he needed to

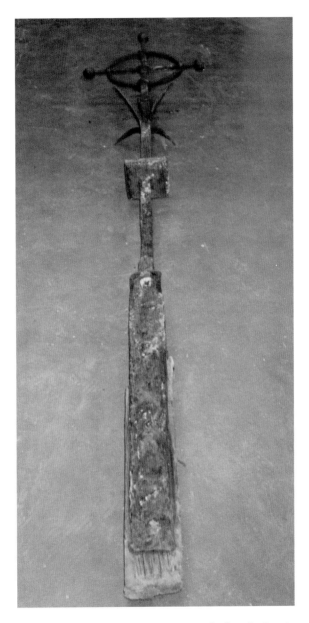

The bell tower cross which was struck by lightning in the winter of 1998

The cross sitting on the ground

learn for the October mod which, unbeknown to himself, he frequently would sing while he worked.

Very few of the rest of the workforce could speak Gaelic. But by the time of the end of the contract, all our workmen could virtually sing the songs required, word-perfect, to compete in the Mod.

By now we were expecting our first visit from the architect, and more importantly a visit from the quantity surveyor, whose job it was to measure up the work we had done to date, and all the material, then issue an interim payment certificate. This would be checked and signed off by the architect and sent to the client for payment which would take a further three weeks.

The architect's visits were held on a monthly basis and I was expected to meet him or his representative at Mallaig, after he had driven up from Ayr the night before, stayed the night in a Mallaig hotel (at the client's expense) and joined me on the Small Isles ferry — the MV *Lochmor* — for the crossing to Canna.

During the summer, depending on which day of the week it was, you could find yourself going direct from Mallaig to Canna. Other days you could find yourself going via the small isles of Eigg, Muck and Rum.

The year 1999-2000 was a very interesting year in the history of these islands; they were soon to lose their flit boat system as it was intended to construct jetties where a roll-on/roll-off ferry could actually tie up to the jetty and offload its cargo by forklift i.e. all the necessary food and fuel supplies required to keep the islands alive until the ferry's next visit.

The system that was used before the jetties were built involved the Lochmor coming into a sheltered loch at each island where she would drop anchor and then a smaller vessel would come alongside. All the ferry cargo for that island would then be lifted off the Lochmor and onto the small passenger boat for its onward journey to the island slipway, where it would be lifted off and into various modes of transport, whether that be an old Landover, a tractor or simply a push barrow. (And we thought we were having multiple handling problems!)

The visitors and island residents were also expected to make the same way ashore, albeit they were not lifted off the deck by crane, but descended a ladder over the side of the Lochmor and onto the smaller boat. This system was reasonably safe in calm weather, but it took great skilful seamanship, by both skipper and crew of each boat, to carry out this tricky manoeuvre on a stormy day, and was deemed dangerous in these years of "health and safety". Hence the £15 million spend on the Small Isles jetties. We were actually very fortunate in 1999 as Canna was the only Small Isle that had a good hard stand jetty where the ferry could tie up alongside.

On reaching Canna, the architect and quantity surveyor were taken to the farm house where they had organised half board with Wendy. I, meanwhile, would make my way to the site and discuss with our foreman, joiner and mason, any issues which needed to be covered at the site meeting with the architect next morning.

Normally, on previous jobs, the architect's visit only lasted half a day but our architect's visits were to last until the next ferry came in to take him off the island; some of them, therefore, lasted three days.

On his first visit to our camp he was full of praise for what we had achieved to date and it was after an inspection of our office accommodation that he christened it the Horizontal Hilton.

Now that St Edwards was completely surrounded by scaffolding, the architect could carry out a close investigation of the upper areas of the structure and instruct us which defective parts of the building were to be removed. A lot of time was spent discussing the condition of the heat-damaged top stonework of

The *Lochmor* unloading the island provisions onto the Rum flit boat

The Eigg flit boat (small passenger ferry)

Eigg jetty

The damaged brick bell tower arches

the bell tower. The result was that we were to remove four of the upper sandstone lintels, re-bed them in a lime cement mix and completely replace the cracked lintels. We also had to replace the central ornamental sandstone mullion and carefully dismantle three of the brick arches and then rebuild them.

Rebuilding the bell tower arches was no problem, as most of that type of material was now on site. What was a problem, as we had discovered at tender stage, was obtaining the specialised building items that were required to restore a 100-year-old building; not the type of materials you could get by simply walking into a builder's merchants and picking up off the shelf. Likewise for the replacement sandstone lintels and the ornamental sandstone mullion.

A sandstone sample would have to be taken back to Kyle at the end of the first trip and sent off to our preferred ornamental stone mason who was based in Caithness. He in turn would have to match the sandstone to a quarry that could supply an identical replacement stone, which just happened to be found in the Midlands. The stone was then cut to the required size, transported back to Caithness, where it would be carved as per our samples, and transported back to Mallaig where it would be loaded onto the *Lochmor* for its final journey out to Canna. We estimated that with the length of time it would take, it would be three months before we could start rebuilding the bell tower.

Johnnie, our machine operator, and his team were now excavating the new road which ran close to Point House, which had been in the original contract and was intended to be the accommodation for the new manager and his family. We had identified suitable road building material in two separate locations on Canna, quite close to the site, but although during each storm hundreds of tonnes of this road material was getting washed into the sea, we were not allowed to use any of it. The client insisted all materials had to be shipped in.

Johnnie is a person who speaks his mind if he does not like you; he is only too quick to tell you.

While he was excavating for the new road up to StEdwards Chapel, we came across a very soft section of ground, which the road had to cross. This soft section had to be removed as it was not capable of taking heavy vehicles. This involved digging down five feet to the rock. While carrying out this excavation the mini-excavator threw a track. Johnnie was not amused, and shouted at me: "Look at what has happened. This is the third time this track has come off today. What are you going to do about it? You should have left this pile of scrap at home and brought the JCB 3CX."

When I tried to explain to him that the reason I had decided to take the lighter tracked machine and not a wheeled machine, was for its versatility. My reason fell on deaf ears.

Johnnie said: "You are not working these machines! You should have left that decision to me."

We kept the large rough-terrain telehandler on Sanday, and left the smaller Toyota forklift on Canna pier for ourselves and Packie to use to unload future deliveries from the *Lochmor*.

When the new access road was completed, the architect complained that it was the wrong colour. We had used material from a quarry on the Isle of Skye but in the architect's eyes it was too white. I explained to him that with the tractor and trailer frequently driving over the road, the surface would soon get dirty, and would no longer look too white. He, however, was having none of it. I also told him that to be a good restorer, the contractor should make every effort to source the material required within a 25-mile radius, and that the road material had been sourced from a quarry that was less than 10 miles away. He was still not happy and insisted the road would need a further coat of grey crusher

Mini-excavator with the thrown track

New access road at various construction stages

New access road at various construction stages

The road hammerhead being formed at the gable end of St Edwards

dust, to cover the white material we had used. He also said that the National Trust for Scotland was not prepared to accept the road owing to its colour. This was something I struggled to accept when I found on a later visit to Canna the NTS had used the same white material to repair the Farm access road.

Although we were now looking at a possible three month delay in terms of rebuilding the bell tower, there was plenty to get on with inside; however, we were losing valuable calm weather and the nights were getting darker with winter closing in fast.

We had brought slaters in from Inverness to strip the existing slates off the main roof. They confirmed the slates were Easdale slates and that they had been nailed onto the roof using bronze nails. That type of slate is quarried on the island of Easdale from where the slates take their name. As the crow flies, Easdale is not very far away from Canna and when you think about it, it made a lot of sense as both the source and the destination were islands, which would have meant the original builders could get the slates to the site by boat, although it is not the best slate in Scotland, owing to its pyrites. Pyrites is a gold colored type of poor quality metal, commonly known as fool's gold, which runs through the slate. This metal could absorb moisture and rust, weakening the slate when used on roofs exposed to severe weather.

It was our job to find replacement, second-hand Easdale slates, because the quarry on Easdale Island where the original slates came from had closed, leaving only second-hand slates available. However, owing to the pyrites, the slate becomes very brittle and inclined to break when it is being stripped off old roofs. In fact, this is what was happening on the roof of St Edwards; the minute the slaters went near the slates with the stripping irons, they were breaking.

Eventually we sourced second-hand slates, which the architect was happy with, in Glasgow and arranged for them to be

The Sanday mode of transport

Annie and Ross sitting on the Horizontal Hilton steps discussing progress

sent to Kyle for the *Highland Carrier's* second load. Because of insufficient deck space on the first trip we made, the *Highland Carrier* had to return with further materials and equipment. It had made no difference how often we had juggled our load around the ship's deck, we were not able to get everything on, and the ship's mate had eventually said: "Enough is enough!" So it made sense to wait for the replacement slates to be delivered to Kyle, before sailing with this load to Canna.

When the slates finally arrived on site they had to be taken out of their crates and sized. Once the old slates had been stripped off the roof we were able to assess the condition of the roof timbers. The sarking was in amazingly good condition, considering the age of the roof, and was only rotten near the gable walls. The roof joist ends though, were rotten where they cantilevered over the stone walls, where they'd had less protection from the elements. The slaters also found that it was virtually impossible to recover the ornamental ridge without breaking the first three top courses of slates. I could not authorise this, as it was in our contract to "salvage all original materials as carefully as possible". We would have to wait for the architect's visit as he was not prepared to make such a decision over the phone without first seeing the problem.

Now that the roof was completely bare of protection we had to cover it with plastic sheeting, to prevent the rain from getting into the chapel and causing any further damage. Once this was done we could get on with the task of removing the existing floor, as it was extremely dangerous to walk on given its rotten state, which we needed to do in order to lay the new concrete floor to access and remove the christening font and the marble communion table. Like the bell, these were to be carefully dismantled, crated up and transported to the new chapel down at the farm house.

The font

The marble table

The arched entrance doors

When we came to dismantle these valuable pieces of religious furniture, we could not believe the weight of them and could only marvel at the way the workmen would have brought them into the chapel 100 years ago, especially through such a narrow entrance door, which was barely wide enough for the items themselves to pass through, far less with the number of men that would have been required to move them. The timber floor would certainly not have been strong enough to roll the units in on.

After the floor boards were inspected by the architect and found to be unsuitable for reuse, Duncan, the joiner, used them to construct duck boards, which were laid on the ground between the chapel and the Horizontal Hilton to stop the mud getting in, owing to all the to-ing and fro-ing.

The architect had full board accommodation with Wendy, over at Canna farmhouse, which included a packed lunch he would bring along on the morning of his site visits.

To be seen to be "one of the boys" the architect would join us all in the Horizontal Hilton dining room for lunch; when he saw all the fresh baking on offer, his lunch bag was quickly set aside.

His eyes turned to Duncan who is a big man, six foot six and over twenty stone.

"Does that man do twice the work of everyone else?" he asked. "Why do you ask?" I said, to which he replied: "He seems to eat twice as much as everyone else; it must be costing you a fortune to keep him."

Our contract included for the necessary repairs to the beautiful arched entrance door and restoring the door hinges and box lock. The term box lock is given to the large lock that is fitted to the inner face of the door, and actually looks like a box stuck on the door — hence the name. These were removed and sent off for restoration. The lock cost £400 to restore and each of the two new keys cost £75.

The stained glass windows were also to be removed and replaced. These delicate leaded units were loaded up in to specially made crates, returned to the mainland and sent off to Aboyne to be restored by Martin, who would then arrange for their return and come on site himself to fit the more tricky unit as we did not have the necessary expertise within our island work force to refit this very valuable glazing.

To ensure the chapel remained wind and watertight, we boarded up the window openings with plywood, making it even darker inside.

The outside work had not quite come to a complete stand-still and now that the architect had identified the faulty pointing we were able, by hammer and chisel, to remove the defective cement pointing between the natural stones. These stones had been quarried on Canna, dressed by the stonemasons 100 years before and then used as the raw material to build the chapel.

The actual quarry where the stone came from could be seen from the second scaffolding tower level. On close inspection of the quarry face you could still see the bore holes, which would have been bored by hand to accommodate the necessary quantity of explosives to blow the stone off the rock face.

We spent the next month picking out the hard cement pointing around the facing stone on each of the four external wall elevations of the bell tower. Once we had done this, we awaited the architect's next visit for further instruction.

When he next arrived, and after inspecting the pointing that had been taken out, he instructed us to remove all the existing pointing. This was a major blow as we had only taken enough cement lime and pointing sand to carry out the repairs that we had been asked to price on the original bill of quantities. The architect's instruction now meant that we would have to arrange another shipment as the quantity required was greatly in excess of the material we presently had on site.

We had already been informed by Cal Mac that they were willing to assist in delivering small quantities of material to us but were unable to deliver larger loads as, for no other reason than their tight schedules, it simply did not allow for the time involved in loading and unloading.

After the pointing blow, the architect dropped a further bombshell; he also wanted all of the plaster on the internal walls removed — throughout the entire building! None of this work had been mentioned in the original tender documents. He then wanted the protective covers removed from the roof so he could inspect the joists. Afterwards he told us to remove the first three lengths of sarking round the entire length of the roof to expose the cantilevered roof joists, and to individually number the joists, to distinguish which was completely rotten and in need of replacement, and which could be repaired by cutting out the rotten section and splicing in a new piece.

We started the repointing on the first areas we had prepared, which had been inspected by the architect. We were not at all happy with his specification mix or the procedure he wanted us to use to apply the new pointing.

We had left a skeleton workforce in Kyle who were working on contracts with our local clients, one of which was the five year winter repairs and renovations to Eilean Donan Castle at Dornie and which involved carrying out similar works, repointing external stone walls, although they were in a less exposed climate than St Edwards Chapel.

The Eilean Donan Castle contract was being run by an architect who was born and brought up on the west coast of Scotland and who seemed to have a better awareness of our winter weather conditions and wind strengths. He was also prepared to

The numbered roof joists and the rotten cantilevered joists

The numbered roof joists and the rotten cantilevered joists

listen to experienced tradesmen, who also were well used to working on buildings in exposed locations.

The specification and procedure we were given to carry out the pointing repairs in Canna were completely different, and our masons were pretty unhappy doing the job with this new lime-mix, using this alien procedure — so much so that a letter was written to the architect, spelling out our feelings.

Sending a letter to an architect, questioning his instructions, is not something you do without a great deal of forethought because architects, as a whole, do not like to be questioned, far less be told that they might actually be wrong. The architect holds the purse strings on the contract as it is his final signature you require on the client's payment certificate to get your next pay cheque for work you have carried out over the last month.

As we anticipated, our letter was quickly swept under the table, and we were told to carry out the pointing as instructed, whether we liked the procedure or not. I remember thinking at the time that the architect's arrogance would come back to haunt him.

We were well aware that we had intruded on Canna's normal peace and quiet, so after we got the bulk of our building material off the pier and onto the chapel site, we kept our journeys back and forth to a minimum, although we always chatted if we met any of the local residents.

We were very pleased, therefore, to be invited to Canna's end-of-season barbecue, when all the Canna folk join together for a ceilidh. Were we at last being regarded as part of the island community? Although we doubled the number of mouths to be fed, a good night was had by all and it was a great chance for the team to let off a bit of steam.

During a further visit by the architect, it was decided that the cross on the bell tower roof should be removed and taken back to

The original pointing in the bell tower wall

the mainland for galvanising. This work was to be carried out by Lloyd Engineering. Rick Lloyd assessed the condition of the cross and found that it had originally been forged in a blacksmith's forge, which had caused air spaces between the metal. If dipped in the hot galvanising tanks these bubbles were likely to explode. We brought this latest problem to the architect's attention and were asked for three quotes; one to restore and galvanise the existing cross; one to construct and galvanise a new, similar cross and a third quote to construct a new cross but without the fine detailing metal work of the original. The architect went for option two which meant Rick was to make an identical cross, and I mean identical, right down to the last blacksmith's hammer mark. When it was finished, it was to be sent to Elgin for galvanising, before being brought to Canna.

The decision to replace the cross would mean a delay in finishing the tower itself as the cross would have to be fixed on both sides of the king rafter truss, then stick out through the roof sarking. Therefore, it was important to get the cross back to Kyle as soon as possible.

I thought that perhaps one of the regular visiting fishing boats that came into Canna might take the cross to Mallaig harbor for us, in order to save time by not having to wait for the next Cal Mac ferry. Not a chance! It was regarded by some fishermen to be very bad luck to carry any type of cross on a fishing boat. In the past I had heard of a person not being allowed on a fishing boat if they had a box of Swan Vestas in their pocket, owing to the picture of the black swan on the front of the box, but I had never heard that carrying a cross was regarded as bad luck.

After Rick had taken his measurements, the old cross lay at our workshop in Kyle for months until the architect rightfully decided that it should be returned to St Edwards and bolted to the inner apse wall. The thinking behind this was that if the cross

**All the parts that Rick formed to make the new cross**

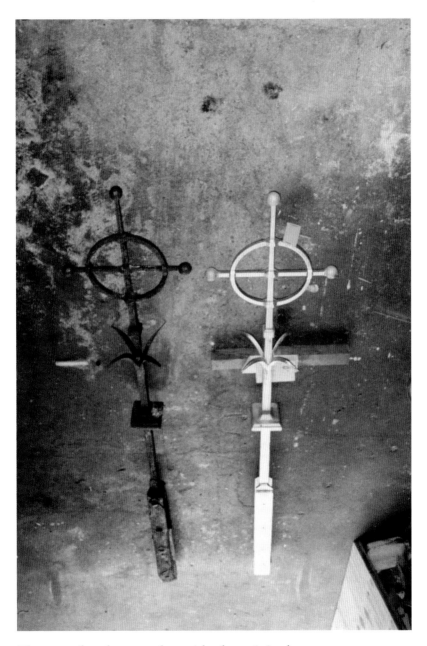

The completed cross, alongside the original cross

hadn't been struck by lightning and the bell tower going on fire there would have been insufficient funds to start the contract.

On one of his later visits, the architect asked me if I would like to join him in an evening visit to meet Mrs Campbell, widow of the late John Lorne Campbell. It was their collection of Gaelic literature, currently housed in Canna House, which was the main purpose for the restoration of St Edwards Chapel.

The intention was for Gaelic students to come to Canna, stay in St Edwards Chapel, and visit Canna House to study this priceless collection of Gaelic stories, poems, songs and other books that John Lorne Campbell and his wife had collected between 1935-1965 on magnetic tape, acetate disc, wire and wax cylinder. Much of their material had been copied onto disc, wire and tape by John, to make working copies. All this reproduction has caused deterioration, with a lot of his early material having to be sent to the National Sound Archive in London for repair, before being made available to the students.

Perhaps some of these students would fall in love with Canna and become part of the community, ultimately being part of the island's regeneration

In 1821 the population of Sanday and Canna was 436, (206 males 230 females), with 53 houses inhabited. In 1891 the population had dropped to 102 people; by 1931 the population had dropped further to 60 and by 1991 it was down to 20 residents on Sanday and Canna.

In 1999, when we working there, Canna and Sanday had a total of 13 people — this included three children in the primary school and one child in pre- nursery. The two older girls would move off Canna to secondary school in Mallaig within the next three years, leaving this fragile community in a very vulnerable position. It was also the intention that St Edwards Chapel would be connected to Sabhal Mor Ostaig, the Gaelic college on Skye, by an ISDN link.

Now in her mid-nineties, Mrs Campbell still lived on her own in Canna House, which she and her late husband had inherited when they bought Canna from Robert Thom's son, Alan G Thom, in 1938.

Despite her age, she was still mentally sound when it came to looking after the interests of her beloved island. She asked me how much water were we intending to use in our cement because did I know that Canna suffered from a water shortage? Although by that point the supply had been virtually replaced, and for the first time ever St Edwards had a good water pressure, Canna no longer really had the water shortage that had plagued it for years. But that is not the point; here was a woman in her nineties who still had her beloved island right in the centre of her heart.

Mrs Campbell had been born in Pennsylvania, in the US, the youngest of five sisters, and she lost her mother at the age of seven. Thereafter Margaret was brought up by her father and her aunts. Tragically she was to lose her father five years later. This orphaned daughter of a Pittsburg steel working family was very unsettled after losing both her parents at such a very young age, and struggled to settle in the various boarding schools she was sent to in the Pittsburg area. A minister friend of her parents, Dr Hugh Hodge, had left America with his family to spend three years in Scotland, and he contacted Margaret's uncle, her guardian, to suggest she join their own daughter in attending a boarding school in Helensburgh. Margaret's uncle was not happy at the thought of sending this very young girl such a long distance on her own and it was a neighbour called Aunt Toni Hartwell who changed her uncle's mind by saying it was a chance of a lifetime and that it would be good for Margaret. A passage was booked for her to sail from New York to Glasgow, but someone would have to be found to be Margaret's guardian during the passage, owing to her very young age. Her uncle obtained the passenger sailing list and contacted a Mrs Brothers who lived in Pittsburg, who was also sailing on the same trip, and she agreed to look after Margaret during the long voyage.

Margaret's sister took her to New York to join the ship, the SS *Columbia*. The young girl was greatly impressed with the *Columbia* as it had three funnels. It was from the Anchor Line based in Glasgow and had a Scottish crew. During the passage over to Scotland, one of the ship's crew brought a bird to Margaret, which had landed on the deck of the ship. This large black and white bird which no one could identify was identified by Margaret years later as a Manx Shearwater, many of which are seen around her home in Canna.

The ship's first port of call on reaching the British Isles was Lough Foyle in Ireland. After dropping off some passengers she then sailed to Scotland, round the Mull of Kintyre and up the River Clyde to Glasgow. On sailing up the river Clyde Margaret was greatly impressed with the shipbuilding taking place on both sides of the river.

The *Columbia* docked at the Broomielaw, in the centre of Glasgow, and from there Margaret continued her journey by horse and cart to her new boarding school. Her interest had always been in music for which she had developed a taste while listening to her older sister being taught the piano by a German professor in Pittsburg. It was while studying in Scotland that she fell in love with the Gaelic language, initially through music. This love came about when she heard a tinker busking with his bagpipes in the back garden of her boarding school, dressed in an old army coat.

Margaret was very happy at school in Scotland and settled in well, giving a lot more of her time to her studies. She returned to America after completing her secondary education via a paddle steamer trip down the Caledonian Canal from Inverness. The voyage took her across Scotland, down through Loch Ness into Loch Linnhe and onward to Oban, then south through the Crinan Canal to Ardrishaig. She then changed from the paddle steamer onto the larger MacBrayne ferry to sail for the River Clyde, calling in at Rothesay and Gourock, before finally sailing into Glasgow, where she changed ships and boarded the SS *Cameronia* bound for New York.

But by now, Margaret was smitten with the Scottish way of life, and soon returned to Scotland, on holiday, pursuing Gaelic songs and stories. She started to cycle round Scotland and ended up in North Uist in the Outer Hebrides. While there she endeavoured to mingle with the local people and gain their trust. The only way she thought she could do this was to actually live with the local people of the Uists. She lived with a family for five years. It was while living with this family in their thatched cottage that she learnt to speak Gaelic.

During her years with the family, Margaret started to record the way of life by photographing them at work and play. She listened to the tales and songs with great interest and soon realised that these great stories and songs were being handed down, from one generation to the next, by word of mouth; very few, if any, were actually written down. She realised that if these songs and tales were not recorded soon, they may be lost forever.

It was then Margaret took on her life-long task of collecting what material there was, writing it down and recording it all. Her work soon took her down through the Uists and onto Barra, where she met Compton Mackenzie, another writer who had heard of the shipwreck tale of the SS *Politician*, and its booty of whisky. It was he who wrote, in 1946, the tale of 'Whisky Galore'.

For whatever reason Margaret never felt at home with the Barra people and returned to South Uist. It was while she was back in Lochboisdale, South Uist that she met John Lorne

Campbell, a member of the gentry who was also learning, studying and recording the Gaelic language. They married in Glasgow in 1935 and after their years in the Uists, they moved to Ireland to continue their Celtic studies.

In 1938 John and Margaret Campbell bought Canna, where John continued to support the farm, building up its herd of pure thoroughbred Highland cattle. They then moved into Canna House, bringing their vast collection of Gaelic literature with them.

John never imposed his lairdship on the people of Canna, realising that they knew better than him how to survive on such a remote Scottish island. John and Margaret also spent several holidays in Italy, and sadly while on holiday there, visiting a monastery in 1996, John passed away. He had left a wish, to be buried wherever he fell and Margaret kept his wish; John Lorne Campbell was buried in Italy.

Fortunately for Margaret, during the holiday they had met a very loyal friend, Magda, who came to Margaret's aid and escorted her back to Canna. When we went out to Canna in 1999, Magda was still living there. We would regularly meet her in the mornings, cycling down to Canna House to assist Margaret with her daily chores. Also while in Canna House, Magda started to catalogue the vast Gaelic collection John and Margaret had accumulated over their 60 years. It was sadly not until their latter years that John and Margaret were recognised for their life-long works in preserving and recording the Gaelic language.

By now winter was closing in, but before it did we had some unexpected visitors. My friend Douglas, who had been out with me on my first site visit, came over in his speed-boat but prior to leaving Kyle, he had telephoned my wife Annie and asked her if there was anything we desperately needed. "Yes," said Annie, "toilet rolls!" There would have been a very unhappy workforce in Canna if the Horizontal Hilton had run out that particular necessity.

Much to our envy, Douglas's trip from Kyle only took him one hour and 25 minutes, whereas our trips from Kyle were taking on average six and a half. We would leave Kyle at 8.30am by minibus, drive over the Skye Bridge and down through south Skye to Armadale, catch the Cal Mac ferry to Mallaig and the onward journey via Eigg, Muck, and Rum to Canna. We would not get our feet on dry land in Canna until 3.30pm in the afternoon whereas Douglas completed the trip in only one-and-a-half hours, as long as it was a calm day.

As well as Douglas, we also had a visit from Alistair in his Princess — the man who had been responsible for my first ever visit to Canna back in June 1995, when we had set off but not arrived at St Kilda. Alistair was actually good enough to bring out a new bench saw and to go via Mallaig to pick up the architect's representative for his regular visit. The workmen were delighted to see the saw although I couldn't say the same about the other item of cargo that he brought out.

With the winter came the short days and by now we only had about one hour of daylight left by the time we arrived on our first day back of each trip. Consequently, not only was the generator now illuminating the Horizontal Hilton, it also had to light up the works outside and inside the chapel; for the first time in its long life, St Edwards Chapel had light inside it. Were we now bringing history together! Robert Thom, the owner of Canna in 1886, had given the Marquess of Bute a remote but prominent site on Sanday to build a chapel with a bell tower that might act as a lighthouse. Now there was a light in the chapel bell tower.

With this extra workload the generator was now consuming a far greater quantity of diesel than had originally been allowed for and at this rate of consumption we would run out of fuel before the contract was completed. It had been my intention to run the site during the day with the other small 7kva generator we had taken with us, but this smaller generator was being powered by a very noisy engine, which was very irritating to listen to all day. After the workmen had had to listen to it for a few days they refused to switch it on and subsequently the large generator was used all day. It was shut down when the last man went to bed, a procedure which was very interesting to watch. In the evening all the workmen would be in the Horizontal Hilton lounge watching TV and as the evening went on, slowly, one by one, the workmen would start making their way to their beds until the last two or three were left. Because it was the duty of the last man up to go out and switch the generator off, there would be a bit of a race to get to bed as, with all the power off and no lights that poor soul would have to make his way to his bed by torchlight. This was nothing new for the islanders though, as we found when we were staying in the shepherd's cottage.

Packie was in charge of the island generator, which powered all the houses on the island, so when he decided it was time for bed, everyone had to go to bed. Whether they liked it or not, all the power went off at the same time. The island had used this system for years to save fuel.

As it was the last man to bed who switched the power off, so it was the first man up who had to go out and switch it on, at which point the noise and the lights woke everyone up, whether they liked it or not. This reminded me of the same problem all those months before when I was with Alastair on his Princess and he would make his first cup of tea of the day.

The bad weather was beginning to affect the *Lochmor* sailing times and each Monday before we left Kyle we would have to telephone the Cal Mac office to enquire whether the car ferry was sailing from Armadale to Mallaig and whether it would carry on to Canna. One late November for the first time during our stay, the *Lochmor*, owing to the poor weather conditions, did not turn up in Canna on the Wednesday afternoon. That news did not go down well with the workforce and two of the younger workmen and our cook, Anne, ended up arranging a lift back to Mallaig on a fishing boat that had called in to Canna that same day for shelter until the weather improved, leaving the rest of the workforce on the island without a cook, although she had prepared sufficient meals for the men before she left.

The remainder of the team was stuck on Canna till the Friday when the *Lochmor*, after the storm had abated, made a special run to Rum and Canna to deliver the Wednesday cargo and pick up the waiting passengers from both islands.

As I was back in Kyle at this time dealing with the rest of our contracts, I was confronted with a none too pleased workforce on the Friday, asking what I was going to do about the situation if it happened again. Well, what could I say? Good as I might be at some things, I was not in control of either the Cal Mac skippers or the weather. Looking back on it now, that was the start of the friction in the Horizontal Hilton. If not, it was the start of the problem that followed soon thereafter.

On the next trip out, we experienced the same problem; the *Lochmor* did not turn up in Canna on the Wednesday, nor the Friday. By the Friday, the cook was going frantic, panicking that the Hilton was going to run out of food. Fortunately Annie had foreseen this very problem and had filled the larder with tinned meat, fruit and vegetables, as an emergency ration pack if and when we might require it. So there was food, albeit not fresh.

There was now only one more 10-day trip scheduled before Christmas and the boys were concerned that the ferry might not turn up to take them back on the Wednesday. If I could not give them a guarantee that they would definitely get off Canna for Christmas, then they were not prepared to go on the last working trip of the year.

Troubled, I went back to PDG Helicopters and asked for an updated quote, so that, if all else failed, the helicopter could bring them back home. Although I had not been able to accept their earlier quote for regular transportation on and off the island, they were only too grateful to assist, although the price had gone up; they were now charging £950 + VAT for the round trip, and only allowed five minutes down time on Canna, for all the men to get into the required survival suits. I knew the workmen wouldn't believe the cost but they would believe, if push came to shove, the helicopter was capable of flying in all weathers and they would get off Canna for Christmas.

It was soon upon us and we closed down the Horizontal Hilton, turned off the water to the site, tied down everything that could be tied down in case of wild weather and returned home for a three-week break.

When the workmen and cook returned to Canna on 19th January they found that the festive gales had ripped off part of the roof covering on one of the portable cabins; however, they were not too worried as the damaged roof was over the boss's office and bedroom. However, there were some other problems; the cook, my sister, had had enough and left the site halfway through the first trip of the new year.

The men struggled on, catering for themselves until the end of the trip but by now, as well as our own workmen staying, we also had subcontractors — electricians and plumbers — residing in the Horizontal Hilton. I had to find a replacement cook, and fast. If not, the job would come to a complete standstill. Knowing exactly how much was at stake my wife Annie, at a moment's notice, came to my aid yet again and agreed to come to Canna to carry on the cooking. Although she had a fear of the sea and bad weather, she upped sticks and came out, where she remained until the end of the contract.

By now we thought we had experienced the worst of the winter gales, but what Annie and the workmen had to experience over the months of January and February was horrendous. I remember one trip when the *Lochmor* got as far as Rum, then turned back, with all its passengers still onboard, which meant Annie and the boys went back to Kyle and all the food had to be unpacked into our fridge and freezer at home, only to be repacked the next morning in the hope the boat would sail.

On another trip back from Canna to the mainland, we were waiting with the minibus in Armadale for the *Lochmor* to come alongside the pier, when, at the last minute, the skipper turned the boat around and headed for Mallaig. We can only presume in his opinion it was unsafe to come alongside Armadale pier. That last-minute decision by the skipper now meant a further return journey of 240 miles by minibus. We would have to go back through Skye to Kyle and then on to Fort William, where we would rendezvous with the Mallaig train which, to save more lost time, the workmen would take. To crown it all, the minibus had a puncture on the way back from Fort William to Kyle which meant that instead of Annie and the boys getting home at 6.00pm they finally got home at 10.00pm. This, sadly, was not the last trip Annie and the workmen would make home by road from Mallaig. If the Small Isles ferry was running slightly late on its arrival back into Mallaig, Cal Mac would not hold back the last day sailing to Armadale even although they knew that there were at least eight passengers needing this onward connection. On more than one occasion, I remember us on the *Lochmor* having to wait outside Mallaig harbour until the Skye car ferry cleared its berth. This being the last ferry to Skye, we were now stranded in Mallaig which meant looking for overnight accommodation. Of course, unlike the architect, we had to cover the cost ourselves. It was at times like this that the PDG quotation looked like a bargain.

These delays, which were completely out of our control, were brought to the architect's attention when he would frequently ask at the monthly meetings what was delaying the work programme but of course, again it fell on deaf ears.

When the workmen finally got onto Canna, there was plenty of inside work to be getting on with. We started to strip the internal plaster off the walls. Again our senior mason questioned our having to undertake this task. Alby, who is not a man of many words, said: "The plaster we were chiseling off the walls is far superior to the new plaster specified to replace it."

Once again we brought this observation, made by an experienced tradesman, to the architect's attention and once again the comments fell on deaf ears.

We also started to lay the foundations for, and build, the brick walls to form and support the spiral concrete access stair to the two floor levels. There were no external fire escapes permitted on the outside of this listed building, therefore these stairs were the escape from the upper levels and had to be constructed with a fire-proof material, and be enclosed by fireproof walls, so that in the event of a fire, safe exit would be given by the internal stair. The only other escape from the bedrooms was by climbing out the yet-to-be-installed mock-Georgian escape skylights.

This form of exit always puzzled me. Were you expected to climb out onto the roof, slide down, and then jump the 20 feet to the ground and hope you would not break both your legs, to escape a fire? Well I dare say that option is better than being burnt to death!

Finally, and after a wait of over four months, the sandstone lintels and central column were ready for dispatch from the north of Scotland and we arranged for the sandstone to be delivered direct to Mallaig. I would meet the sandstone there and supervise the off loading from the truck and onto the Lochmor.

When the sandstone finally got to Canna it was immediately

loaded onto our tractor and trailer, and as the tide was out, we got it directly on the site. The boys had always been insistent that I should be on site to supervise this long-awaited and very valuable material into its final position, three floors up the bell tower.

When we built the scaffold we incorporated a stronger loading section into the middle of it for this very job. With the aid of a chain block we gently lifted the sandstone lintels into their final position.

The reason we used the chain block instead of the rope, block and tackle was because we were now handling a far heavier load and the chain pull was more controllable, allowing us to stop and start.

The sandstone lintel being loaded onto the *Lochmor* in Mallaig

The sandstone lintel being lifted up the scaffold with the aid of a chain block

CHAPTER FIVE

# Completing the restoration of Listed Building

With the first sandstone lintel now in place, and the darkness closing in, we decided to call it a day. The next morning was spent lifting the remaining two lintels, and the sandstone ornamental central column, up the scaffold and lifting them all into place. Lifting the lintels by hand onto the top of the bell tower walls involved three men standing on the inside scaffold and another three men standing on the outside scaffold, working as a team and all lifting at the same time.

We looked around in wonder and tried to imagine how this operation was carried out 100 years ago, when those hardy workmen would not have had all the mechanical aids available to them that we have today.

Unfortunately although I carried out an extensive search I was unable to find any information about the skilled craftsman who actually cut the stone from the quarry face, dressed it and laid the mortar and stone to build St Edwards Chapel, which is a great shame. But, sadly, this seems to be the way in the building construction industry — the people who actually carry out the hard graft seem to be the ones who receive least recognition.

But what I did unearth was that William Frame, the architect who had carried out a lot of design work for the Bute family, both at Cardiff Castle and at Mount Stewart, had been dismissed on several occasions, owing to a personal problem, before being reinstated to design and supervise the building of St Edwards Chapel.

Frame designed the building for Lady Bute, rather than for the islanders, or the Diocese. Records show that there were problems, due to the architect's unfamiliarity with the climate and the local building materials used.

With the lintels finally bedded into position, we could now concentrate our efforts on rebuilding the fire-damaged brick arches.

When the mortar was set on the newly-built arches, we rebuilt the stone wall head, and bedded on the new wall plate to take the new timber roof. I make no apology for giving all the measurements on this job in feet and inches. This is the measurement that was used to construct this beautiful building and the specification dictated that all the timbers we removed had to be set aside for inspection by the architect and the various conservation bodies who had an interest in this restoration, before being measured in feet and inches and replaced by us.

We had managed to salvage part of one of the fire-damaged roof trusses that was on the bell tower, which enabled us to construct an identical replacement. When the architect had inspected and noted the sizes of timbers used on the original construction, then any time we went back down to the pier we would take a load of wood down to Winnie or Packie, as firewood was in very short supply on an island that had very few trees, especially dry sticks, to light the fire.

On completion of the roof truss we lifted the king truss onto the new timber wall plate, with the chain hoist.

After securing it into position we could construct the remainder of the roof joists then cover the roof with the timber

The original workforce on St Edwards Chapel (Mrs J.G.Sewell)

The damaged ornamental central column and its new replacement

The new sandstone lintels

The newly-formed roof truss, before and after, being lifted into position

The bird beak joint used 100 years ago and reproduced by Duncan, our joiner, to stop the roof joist slipping on the cross tie beam

The galvanised splicing plates in various locations on the repaired roof timbers

The galvanised splicing plates in various locations on the repaired roof timbers

The galvanised splicing plates in various locations on the repaired roof timbers

The morticed replacement timber roof ties

sarking. Before fully covering the roof, we left a section above the king rafter, to enable us to install the new cross when it returned to site. With the bell tower now complete, we could concentrate on splicing the identified main roof joists' timbers, strengthening them with galvanised side plates.

The main roof was resarked and felted to make it watertight, protecting the internal vaulted ornamental plaster ceiling. We then took on a specialist firm to fit the new lightning conductor system. This involved running a copper strip along the ridge of the main roof and down both gables then along to the new cast iron skylights, before finally connecting the copper strips to the new cast iron rhones when they were finally fitted. The same procedure was used on the bell tower roof, except instead of connecting it to the skylights, we ran the copper strip up to the top of the new cross. All these copper strips were then led down the building and connected to an earthing stake that had been driven three feet into the ground.

To comply with new safety regulations, we also had to fit five roof anchors, three of which had to be fitted on the bell tower roof. The remaining two had to be fitted on the main chapel roof behind the bell tower. The purpose of the roof anchors is so that future roof maintenance workmen could secure their roof harnesses onto the anchors which, in the event of the ladder falling, the workman would be restrained.

These roof anchors had to be drilled through the sarking and bolted onto the side of the roof joist. As the weather was beginning to improve we were keen to get the slaters back on site to reslate the roof. Before this could happen, though, the plumbers would have to replace all the lead work on the roof and nail the new stainless steel rhone brackets onto the new sarking and the cast iron rhones had to be replaced.

To do this, we had to take a timber template from the original rhone and a timber template from the curve, round the apse roof. As with previous materials, we found you could not buy these rhones and down pipes from just any plumbing merchant. We had to send the rhone samples and templates to a metal foundry in the Midlands so a sand cast could be made, into which molten cast iron would be poured to form the new rhones and down pipes.

We also had to carry out a similar process with the replacement back gate and posts. We took several photographs and gave several measurements of the front entrance gate before having the new one cast by a foundry in Bo'ness.

The slaters were out with us on the next trip and started sizing the slates by individually measuring each one, putting them into similar sized piles and carrying them on their shoulders up the roof. The slaters were asked by the architect to nail them onto the roof using the same number of slate courses that were on the original roof. But this time the slates were to be nailed with galvanised nails and not bronze, as had been originally used.

The slaters were expected to use 16-inch slates on the first three courses, showing seven inches of each slate, then six courses of 15-inch slates showing six-and-a-half inches of slate. This was followed by 10 courses of 14-inch slates, showing six inches, five courses of 13-inch slates showing five-and-a-half inches, four courses of 12-inch slate with five inches showing and lastly three courses of 11-inch slates showing four-and-a-half inches.

It took us over two weeks to remove all the internal plaster, and on virtually each day Alistair would comment on how hard it was to get the plaster off the walls by hand. The plaster was so hard, and of such density, that it looked like a tanking plaster and not an internal decorating plaster, had been used.

We were not allowed to use any mechanical assistance when removing the plaster because great care had to be taken when stripping round the sandstone dado rails, door facings,

The new rear gate and gateposts

ornamental arches and carved faces, when taking the service pipes and wires between floors; we had to raggle into the stone behind the sandstone dado rails, to avoid damaging or cutting them in any way.

During the entire contract works, these faces caused great numbers of discussions as to what the stone faces symbolised, which I think had been the intention of the chapel's original designer. Finally I think we got the correct answer; the ten stone face carvings were of members of the Marquess of Bute's family, varying in age from the young to the quite elderly.

To enable us to start work on replastering the inside walls we required another boat-load of 20 tonnes of building material uplifted from Kyle and brought out to Canna. This small load did not warrant the cost of hiring the *Highland Carrier* so we used the *Gallus Grafter*, an ex-military tank-carrying landing craft

**The service pipes going behind the sandstone and dado rails**

*The Gallus Grafter* loaded before she left Kyle

capable of holding 30 tonnes of deck cargo which had been modified and fitted with a 14-tonne hydraulic crane. It was based in Fort William and was well used to delivering cargo to Canna. The problem with the *Gallus Grafter* was that she could only travel at seven knots which was half the speed of the *Highland Carrier*, and we would be charged for her time as soon as she left Fort William. Her cargo was mostly made up of renovating plaster, plasterboard, insulation, fuel for the generator, finishing timbers and the new cross, which was crated up for its protection and to hide its identity, just in case we had another superstitious crew on the *Gallus Grafter*.

The fuel on this trip was in two 250-gallon bowsers for easier onward transportation from Canna to Sanday. All I can say about this load is that we were very lucky it was a calm day and there was a good forecast for the following 24 hours when the *Gallus Grafter* left Kyle for Canna, because there was not much free board, meaning the open deck was very close to the water's edge and it would only have taken a small set of waves to completely ruin our cargo.

The *Gallus Grafter* sailed at lunchtime for Canna, and arrived safe and sound at about 9.00pm that night but was unable to start offloading the long-awaited cargo until the tide came in. This was because the top of Canna pier was higher than the *Gallus Grafter's* crane could safely lift to, which meant a further delay.

When the supplies arrived at the chapel the next day, our plasterer was able to get going inside. You could not help but notice Cal Mac very seldom took any cargo off the Small Isles. Only the recycled bottles and aluminium cans came off Eigg, and a few boxes of Packie's lobsters were taken off Canna for the mainland markets. Rum was the only island that exported anything.

During the deer-shooting season, which is the 21st of

October to the 14th of February for hinds and the 1st of July to the 20th of October for stags, the Rum flit boat, the *Rhouma*, would bring out bags of venison, carefully wrapped in hessian, with their returning passengers for the journey to Mallaig. This venison was so expertly wrapped that I don't believe any of the *Rhouma's* passengers knew what cargo was travelling with them.

It was George Bullough who had brought deer onto Rum, shortly after he built Kinloch Castle in 1897, to enable his guests to go shooting. Bullough had inherited Rum from his father, James Bullough, who was a very wealthy businessman from Lancaster. Having made his money in the manufacturing industry, James originally took on the lease of Rum in 1879 and eventually bought the freehold. He then enjoyed the lifestyle of acting the part of the Highland laird.

**The Rum flit boat (the *Rhouma*)**

Rum jetty

At the age of 55, James Bullough got married for the second time to an 18-year-old girl from Stornoway. George was very fond of his new stepmother, who was of a similar age to him and the fondness became evident to his father John. To prevent things getting completely out of control, George Bullough was sent abroad.

On his return he spent his time cruising the west coast of Scotland in his private yacht, the *Rhouma*, and found Loch Scresort, known locally as Rum Bay, to be a very safe mooring for his beloved boat. It was then that he demolished the existing building on the site and built Kinloch Castle, importing 250,000 tonnes of Annan sandstone to build his new home. The work took three years to complete.

After his father's death, George built an impressive mausoleum on the west side of the island to accommodate his father's remains. Was there competition going on between the very rich? 10 years before George built this impressive Greek-style mausoleum on Rum; on the next island — Canna, only 3 miles away — the Marquess of Bute had built St Edwards Chapel and she had incorporated within its design, ten face carvings of members of the family. Or was the competition even bigger?

In 1844, when Sir James Matheson bought the Island of Lewis, he built Lews Castle, a mock-Tudor folly. Meanwhile, on the mainland, in 1860 Sir Alexander Matheson built Duncraig Castle, a fine example of Victorian baronial architecture.

And now in 1897 we have George Bullough building Kinloch Castle.

All these buildings on the west coast of Scotland, all in sheltered sea lochs, and all in very remote locations. Lews Castle was sold in 1918 to Lord Leverhulme who only kept it for five years then gifted it to the people of Stornoway in 1923.

We had now completed the repointing of the external walls, except for the lime putty pointing of the dressed sandstone. Most of the internal first and second floor joists were in position and the flooring had been laid on these joists. When, yet again, the architect dropped a further bombshell. He issued a further instruction to completely repoint the chapel's perimeter drystone wall. The original contract had allowed for 30 feet of the perimeter wall that had fallen down to be rebuilt but no mention was made in the tender to repoint any of the perimeter walls. A drystone wall does not use cement anywhere in its construction, it relies on each stone being keyed into the other, which permits the wall to take movement if the foundation ground, below the wall, were to subside.

But now, pointing the wall with cement, you would strengthen the main structure, but you would lose the wall's capability to move in the event of ground subsidence. Ground subsidence can be caused by undermining; Canna is riddled with miners — rabbits!

There were also thousands of rabbits on Sanday. They had been brought onto the island earlier in the century as a food source; if all else failed and no food supplies arrived by boat for whatever reason, then the island people could still get fresh meat by killing the rabbits. We had also been informed that the island was infested by rats, although we only saw two or three during our stay. In saying that, we were always very careful not to leave any rubbish in or around the Horizontal Hilton and always took our food wrappings and empty tins back to Kyle with us at the end of each working trip.

During the spring of 2000 Canna was invaded by another set of workmen, who were contracted to build a new generator shed at Canna Farm to house the two new generators that would finally give Canna and Sanday 24-hour power all year round. It was intended that St Edwards Chapel was also to be connected to this new power supply.

The reinforcing rods weaving through the stair steps

Easter was fast approaching, and with our internal plaster work taking six weeks to complete, the workmen agreed to take a late Easter holiday. We also wanted to complete the tricky self-supporting spiral concrete stair. To do that we had to first build brick walls up the full height of the main chapel roof and then shutter a spiral round a barrel type shutter. We then had to weave reinforcing rods through each shuttered step before pouring in the concrete.

We had to shutter the first floor and second floor landings, lay a reinforced mat and pour the concrete floors, which were also to house the shower rooms. This work had been started in September 1999, when gale-force winds prevented the workmen from working outside. The stair and landings could only be shuttered and filled in sections, because the first floor landing relied on the strength of the ground floor stair for support. The architect insisted the reinforcing was inspected by an engineer before each concrete pour. These inspections caused lengthy delays so it was not until just before Easter 2000 that we were able to shutter and pour the concrete on the second floor landing thus completing our access to the first floor workstations and second-floor bedrooms. Hence the reason we delayed our Easter holiday. The main entrance stair and new internal plaster would get time to dry and set during our week's holiday.

It had been our intention to use Rick again to form the new metal spiral stair rail, which could only be fabricated on site. However, owing to his health deteriorating since he made the bell tower cross, Rick, although still working in his workshop in Kyle, had to be close to medical assistance. We had two qualified first aiders on site and a qualified fire fighter, but our nearest doctor was on Eigg, and our nearest hospital was on the Isle of Skye. Both were at least one hour away by boat and that only if it was calm weather. Emergency help for Canna was by the coastguard helicopter from Stornoway or by the RNLI lifeboat taking medical assistance out of Mallaig.

On returning to Canna after the Easter holidays there were more men to feed and more food to carry out as we had two blacksmiths with us. But again disaster struck. Our very trusty generator, which had never missed a beat for over nine months and had run for over 19,000 hours, would not supply any electric power which meant no lights, no heating, no hot water, no deep freezes, and no welding.

With all the food carried to site, the workmen ready to start work, the *Lochmor* away from Canna and me in Kyle, what was going to happen?

In the end, Packie came to our rescue; there was an old generator which had been lying out in a field for over two years behind the farmhouse which we could use if we could get it going. With a bit of scavenging around, cleaning out the old fuel and stripping the injectors out of our small standby generator and fitting them to this old salvaged generator, our workmen and the blacksmiths got the generator going, albeit with a substantially reduced output of power than we were used to.

Later that evening, with limited lights and the use of the gas standby cooker, Annie, without complaining, prepared a meal for everyone. It was now of the utmost importance to get the damaged generator repaired. Johnnie brought the generator back to Canna on the next low tide, loaded the generator onto the *Lochmor*, and I met the boat in Mallaig where Cal Mac unloaded it onto my waiting trailer for its onward journey to Inverness. There it was stripped down, new parts ordered, then rebuilt and immediately uplifted for its return journey to Canna. Cal Mac was not happy with our forklift lifting the generator in Canna, onto the *Lochmor*. "Why?" we asked ourselves. The telehandler was capable of lifting, one-and-a-half tonnes and the generator was less than a ton in weight.

There was no time to argue. The generator was required back on site as quickly as possible and if Cal Mac were not prepared to take the generator back, then we would have to find another boat that was. In the meantime we had been getting another load together and its delivery was brought forward. Owing to the weight of this load, we required a larger boat than the *Gallus Grafter* so we hired the *Lyrawa Bay*, a converted car ferry from Shetland that was now used for fish farm work; she had a larger deck space and a larger tonnage capacity.

At the end of the *Lyrawa Bay's* normal working week, we set about loading on the Friday afternoon. The load mainly consisted of the one tonne bags of crusher dust that the architect had been insistent on for the road, more 45-gallon drums of fuel for the generator, the generator itself, the new kitchen units and white goods, plumbing fittings, insulation, the restored stained glass windows and some timber. This would hopefully be the last load coming out to Canna.

We sailed to Armadale on the Friday evening where I and another crew man slept aboard. The skipper who had been good enough to give up his normal Saturday off then went home for the night. Early next morning we sailed for Canna. On arrival we were met by a none too happy workforce, owing to the inconvenience they had to put up with when they were without the 60kw generator, which was quickly taken to the site and reconnected to the Horizontal Hilton by Colin our resident electrician

When I arrived on site with the generator I was able to introduce myself to the blacksmiths, inspect their work and thank them for assisting in getting the temporary generator going. I also discovered that they were now well on with the spiral stair hand rail.

We had employed the services of Martin Farrelly to restore

The loaded *Lyrawa Bay* before she left Kyle

the leaded, stained glass windows. Martin was an amazing tradesman, a small man with a wealth of knowledge. He was completely deaf, having lost his hearing at an early age from meningitis. I was concerned how he would cope when he came on site. We need not have worried, however, as it had been the architect's intention to book Martin into Canna Farm, a more homely environment. Martin, though, was having none of it. He wanted to stay in the Horizontal Hilton with the rest of the workmen. It was more how would we cope working with a deaf man; this was something we had not experienced before.

Martin and his assistant, William, arrived and were made welcome by everyone in the camp. We quickly found that Martin had a great sense of humour. He was keen to share his skills with everyone who showed an interest in his work and when Annie

**The spiral handrail on the stair, which was fabricated on site**

told him that she had attended night classes in stained glass work, Martin spent his evenings showing her his work. He told Annie the colours of the glass used in church restoration works should be as seen in the rainbow — red, orange, yellow, green, blue, indigo and violet — i.e. ROYGBIV which reads Read Over Your Good Book In Violet.

Annie had a very soft spot for Martin as we had nearly lost our own daughter at the age of 13 to meningitis.

Martin communicated a lot by letter, and sent Annie a letter when he returned home to Aberdeen. Part of it reads, "and last but not least, the cook kept us well nourished with super meals, at very regular hours, and always with a smile and some banter, that lightened a longish day, 8am to 10ish".

Whilst the stair and stair landings had completely dried out over our holiday period, the internal plaster had not! Pressure was now on us to complete the partitions in the bedrooms and workstations, as we had programmed the painters from Fort William to be out on the next trip to start filling the plasterboard on the ceilings and walls.

The problem with all this internal building heating that we in the 20th century have grown to insist on is that natural stone-faced buildings are porous and with the difference in temperature inside the building and the damp winter weather outside, when the two differing temperatures meet in the external walls the outside moisture condenses, forms into water, which if being prevented from soaking into the ground by modern dampcourse, is drawn into the building, causes damp patches and throws the paint off the internal plastered walls

This problem was addressed, in days gone by, by fitting the leaded windows on the inside of the outer wall condensation line, allowing the moisture to trickle outside.

The painters were out the next trip and on inspection of the work Ian, the foreman painter, made a comment about the type of plaster used on the internal walls and the problem of the amount of moisture still in it. He also suggested that the internal plaster would take the paint better if it was coated with a waterproof sealer. Again we brought this problem and suggestion to the architect and again it fell on deaf ears.

The architect's suggestion was to bring dehumidifiers onto the site to speed up the plaster drying process and as the architect had specially selected an emulsion, also with breathing qualities, there would be no problem.

In the end the painters had to cut their trip short as they simply refused to paint the damp plaster whether the emulsion paint had breathable qualities or not. Tension was now beginning to rise on the job. Every trip the architect had come on site, the first questions were always: Had we caught up on lost time? and Was the job going to finish on time? Never once did the architect fully reflect on the weather we had had to work with when, some days, far from working high up on the scaffold, we were hardly able to stand outside and other times, for reasons outwith our control, we could not even get onto the island, far less, onto the job to work.

It was noted in May 2000 that a swallow had made its nest in the front porch so we received an architect's instruction that all works in the porch area had to stop till the "chicks have fledged". One minute the architect was getting on to us that progress was slow, the next minute he was telling us not to work in certain areas. But work was progressing well. The heating was now complete on the ground and first floor and the electrical work was complete except for the fitting of the meter, which we couldn't do because the island's new 24-hour supply was being held up,

It was intended that as soon as the new power supply was up and running we would switch the chapel onto the new supply and

The original fireplace was the only source of heating for the entire chapel

reduce the load on our generator, thereby reducing its voracious consumption of diesel.

It was now time to start thinking about what was going to happen to the Horizontal Hilton. We offered it to the client through the architect for no payment. This initially was regarded as a good suggestion. Once again we brought to his attention that, although we had a heavy industrial dehumidifier running all the hours the site generator was running, the plaster was still damp. At our next site meeting we were now discussing floor coverings. The architect then selected the carpets for the bedrooms, carpets in the workstations, quarry tiles in the boiler room and lino flooring with marmoleum border in the kitchen and dining room.

The architect also now informed us that owing to the lack of access for furniture getting up the spiral stair, the wasted space within the bedrooms and the vaulted ceiling, he now wanted all the beds and bedroom furniture to be built on site from MDF. Yet again we found ourselves having to arrange transport for this extra material being requested. By the end of June, with us finally seeing light at the end of the tunnel, the Horizontal Hilton was at its busiest. Along with our own boys we had two plumbers, two electricians, and two painters staying with us.

Yvonne my daughter was home preparing herself for her year out, travelling round the world, and required all the money she could get; so she volunteered to assist her mother with the catering on Canna for six weeks. Far from relaxing with the extra help, Annie decided that Yvonne was more than capable of catering for the men during the daytime

Yvonne had not long started her kitchen duties, when one morning the architect stormed into the Horizontal Hilton, while passing the kitchen door and shouted: "Coffee!"

The bunk beds built into the curved bedroom ceilings

The curved walls forming bedrooms in roof space

**The curved walls forming bedrooms in roof space**

Yvonne said: "Who does that man think he is, does he not have the word please in his vocabulary?"

Annie decided that there was no need for both she and Yvonne in the kitchen all day; she would go out on the site and finish the lime pointing on all the external and internal decorative sandstone.

This was a woman who, as well as not liking stormy weather on the boat, was also scared of heights. But Annie knew that our stone masons had kept putting off this work because they found it too tedious and that if the stonemasons would not do it then who would?

The MDF came out on the *Lochmor*, John the joiner set about constructing the bunk beds and chests of drawers, as per the architect's drawings, in the five bedrooms. With great reluctance the painters started to paint the plaster walls, Duncan the joiner was

Annie wrapped up in her oilskins, pointing the sandstone dressings

Some of her internal pointing on the ornamental sandstone

fitting the kitchen units, and Neil the joiner was hanging all the fire doors. Meanwhile Martin the plumber was fitting the sanitary ware. Still progress was not quick enough for the architect.

It was normal practice that our company always had their summer holidays during the first two weeks of August but I don't think any of the workmen fancied another winter working on Canna so they offered to delay their holidays until the end of September. By the end of August all the internal works were complete, including the painting and the laying of the floor covering. A final inspection was made by the architect of the external roof works and the high level pointing, before we dropped the scaffold, which meant us also releasing the scaffolding clamp from around the bell tower. The scaffolding was then taken to the Canna pier.

The client, through the architect, had by now rejected our offer of the Horizontal Hilton, so it was decided that we would flit into the new chapel bedrooms and remove the Hilton off site, which we always knew was going to be a tricky task. We started to split the units and on lifting the first outer unit (and probably the lightest unit) owing to the very soft ground the forklift support legs started to sink in, putting the forklift at a very dangerous angle. This was now deemed by me to be extremely dangerous. Which left us with no other alternative than to completely dismantle the Hilton and dispose of it on site.

By the second week in September it was confirmed that our return transport back to Kyle had been arranged for Saturday the 30th so it was now time to tidy up and get as much of our equipment, tides permitting, back onto Canna pier. This arrangement we also brought to the attention of Packie. When he then brought to our attention that Canna was to perform its first wedding on the island for over 30 years on the same day and that, although he was happy that we took back some of our equipment and stored it at the back of the pier, we were not allowed to block up either the pier or the road until the church ceremony was over.

The 30th of September was a perfect day weatherwise. With the bride and groom arriving on Canna the evening before and the main bridal party arriving on the day in the specially chartered *Shearwater*, a large passenger boat from Mallaig, the wedding service was held in the Presbyterian Church which had been built by Alan G Thom in memory of his father Robert Thom — a copy of an Irish church building in Glendalough

The furniture in St Columba's had been supplied by a lot of the fishing boats that frequently used Canna pier for shelter and had in the past created graffiti by painting their boat's name on the pier rock face. It had been suggested to the skippers of these boats that instead of causing this unsightly mess on the pier rock face if these boats really wanted to be remembered as a visitor to Canna, that they could each purchase a chair for the church and put a small name plate on the back of their donated chair. What a great idea! We also contributed to the new St Columba's Chapel by constructing the oak hardwood front door.

With the main wedding now well in progress we contacted the *Highland Carrier* to come alongside the pier and at about 5pm we were permitted to start loading all our equipment for our home journey. But where was Annie? I went back up to St Edwards and found her on her hands and knees, scrubbing the linoleum floor leaving the place spotless before finally locking up the front door.

The loading took us till 10pm then Packie, in fine fettle, came down from the wedding with a couple of bottles of spirits and thanked us for all the assistance we had given to the Canna people during our 15-month stay. We in turn thanked him for his assistance after which he cast off our ropes.

Annie tiding up in the new St Edwards kitchen

The Canna workforce – left to right: Duncan Macrae (joiner), Alistair Maclennan (mason), Annie Mckerlich (cook+), Yvonne Mckerlich (assistant cook), Neil Campbell (joiner), Colin and Ian (painters), Kenny (apprentice electrician), Neil Mackay (apprentice mason), Colin Mackintosh (site electrician), Morel Junior (blacksmith), Johnnie Mackenzie (machine operator)

CHAPTER SIX
# The opening of St Edwards by HRH Princess Anne

During our last month of September, when we were taking our equipment off Sanday and back to the Canna pier, we inevitably found ourselves picking up a part return load back to St Edwards Chapel, consisting of hardwood dining room tables and chairs, easy chairs, a television, a fax machine, a video, bed linen, towels, pots and pans, crockery, cutlery, and bed mattresses, which had been specially made for the bunk beds. In total enough of everything for 12 people to live comfortably in St Edwards Chapel.

When we finally left the site we poured the remaining diesel out of our 45-gallon drums to refill the chapel oil tank and as instructed, left the heating on at a low setting. On leaving the chapel we handed the door key to Murdo, who was to be the new caretaker of St Edwards Chapel, until the trust employed someone on a permanent basis.

Within three weeks of us leaving, Murdo detected dampness on the kitchen walls. Well, what did they expect now that we had taken away our dehumidifier, which had required emptying every day when we were there. The architect made a further site visit, and decided that the stone that had been used to build the chapel must be porous.

After discussing the problem with the National Trust, and against their advice, the architect then instructed us to quote for spraying two-thirds of the tower and the entire west elevation of the chapel with a German liquid sealer. We by now had taken all of our equipment and transport off the island. Our quote to contract these extra works was accepted.

John and I returned to site early in November on the new car ferry, the *Loch Nevis*. Cal Mac were well ahead of the game by building this new vessel and introducing it on the Small Isles run, because the new roll-on/roll-off ferry terminals on Rum and Muck were just going out to tender and the roll-on/roll-off terminal on Eigg had not long started. The new pier for Canna however, had not as yet been approved.

To carry out the stone spraying work we had to hire in a 40-foot ladder to reach the high areas of the bell tower. As you can imagine, a 40-foot ladder is extremely heavy to carry two miles from Canna pier to St Edwards Chapel, so when we got to Canna we hired Packie to take our equipment to St Edwards Chapel. To complete the job in safety when John was on the ladder with the 12 foot spray lance, I was on the top of the bell tower feeding out the rope tied to the safety harness onto which John was secured. We had not had an accident on the site all the time we carried out the restoration works, and I certainly did not want one now.

We went back a further three times to carry out more spraying over other areas of the chapel. Our contract had stipulated, that five per cent retention would be withheld from every payment, until completion of the contract, then, two-and-a-half per cent of the retention would be released, leaving the final two-and-a-half per cent to be paid after twelve months.

But, by January 2001, we were still waiting for the payment release of the two-and-a-half per cent. We were also waiting for the payment for the extra wall spraying and although being promised payment on several occasions, nothing had arrived.

This now left us with no other alternative than to refuse to carry out any further works until we were paid in full for all works we had done to date.

The internal paint was showing damp stains which the architect wanted repainted under a snagging item; this was water damage, and hence had nothing to do with the snagging.

It was only then that we were told that the building had to be repainted by March 2001 before the official opening; again we informed the architect that no further works would take place by us or our subcontractors until we had been paid.

By February 2001 and still no payment coming we received, via the architect, an invoice from Murdo for his time mopping up the water in the chapel. Tension was now high between us and the architect.

By April, and still no payment, we found the Island of Canna was under an embargo owing to the foot-and-mouth outbreak in the rest of Britain. We finally received a partial payment on the 17th of April 2001.

On the 7th of April we received a letter from the Hebridean Trust with an invitation to the opening ceremony of St Edwards Chapel. I was horrified that the invitation was only for me and did not include my wife Annie. The reason being given was that, owing to space being tight on the specially-chartered vessel, the Hebridean Trust now had also found that the summer Cal Mac sailings did not allow an all-day visit to Canna on a Tuesday, where you could get on and off the island. I then received a further note suggesting that if I could make my journey over on a RIB (rigid inflatable boat) then the trust would make every effort to accommodate my spouse and some of my workers.

On receipt of the invitation from the Hebridean Trust and

especially with the invitation only being for me, I declined the invitation, and wrote to the architect, informing him that by now we had developed a very bad taste for this job owing to the large sum of money still being owed on this contract.

The architect's reply read: "I note what you write and would urge you to reconsider your decision, as I think it would be both sad and inappropriate if you were not at the ceremony, the more so as the success of the project has been undoubtedly due to yourself, your workforce and the effort and enthusiasm you have put into the project."

After the above letter from the architect we received a further part payment with a promise that any additional painting would be paid for. We sent the painters back to St Edwards Chapel to brush down the stained internal plaster walls and repaint.

I feel very sorry for the Royal Family because everywhere they are invited to go and be part of an opening ceremony their nostrils must be full of a fresh paint smell. We asked all our subcontractors if they would like to attend and we also asked our workmen who had been involved in the restoration works of St Edwards Chapel. I asked Alistair, the Princess owner, if he could take Annie and me out to the opening ceremony and he was more than happy to oblige. I then had to go back to the architect for a further invitation for Alistair. This was declined as he was not part of our workforce. It was Alistair, with his Princess, who had originally introduced me to St Edwards and if I had not fallen for it in 1995 then I certainly would not have taken on the contract.

Our party to attend the royal opening was made up of Annie my wife, Neil our foreman joiner, his son Steven and Alistair and his wife Mary, who were described as being our contract transport advisers. We left Kyle at 8.30am on the 5th of June 2001 and arrived on Canna at noon. The journey took a little longer than usual, owing to the weather. We had left ourselves plenty of time

The Donald Mckerlich & Son party arriving on the beach below Point House with the Princess 388 in the background

for the voyage and their was no sense in giving ourselves a rough passage by ploughing through the waves.

On arrival at the chapel we were met by two marquee tents full of people — all the residents of Canna, including the children, who had been given the day off school.

The rest of the people we had never seen before, apart from 10 or so who had visited the works on a few occasions with the architect.

We discovered that when the Hebridean Trust were deciding on the people to be introduced to Princess Anne, none of those involved in the actual rebuilding were included. I was not annoyed that I had not been included, but I was really annoyed that neither Annie nor Neil were to be introduced to her. I was also extremely annoyed that no member of the Hebridean Trust or the architect came and spoke to us. The only person who acknowledged our presence was the quantity surveyor. How rude, considering how welcome Annie had made the architect and any of his guests when they had visited the site. It was as if we were invisible.

HRH the Princess Royal arrived by helicopter and was introduced to the party of people who had been gathered by the Hebridean Trust. She then officially opened St Edwards Study Centre, as it was now to be known, before being presented with three of Packie's lobsters by his daughter Caroline. It was only when Princess Anne then asked to be introduced to the builder that we were given any recognition.

I had been fortunate to have met her back in 1990 when she opened the Lochalsh and Skye swimming pool in Kyle and, like then, she had done her homework on the building she was opening. She asked Annie and me several questions about the reconstruction work. When I started explaining to her the condition of St Edwards, on our arrival on Canna, she said she

Princess Anne arriving by the royal flight.

had actually seen St Edwards with sheep and cattle sheltering in it when she had popped in during one of her many sailing holidays on the west coast.

It was obvious from the look on their faces that the Trust representatives had known nothing of Princess Anne's previous visits to the island.

There was one island resident who was unable to attend the royal opening, owing to her infirmity, and that was Mrs Campbell. After the official opening of the centre was over, Princess Anne lifted off from Sanday and flew over to Canna House by helicopter, a flight that took less than a minute, and there she met the late John Lorne Campbell's widow.

At the age of 101, in 2004, Margaret passed away and was buried on her beloved South Uist; 10 years after his death, John's body was exhumed from Italy in 2006 and his remains were re-buried in Canna.

Their entire collection of Gaelic literature is now in the hands of the Hebridean Trust on Canna, where, hopefully, it will remain intact. To give you some idea as to the quantity of Gaelic material, that was in John and Margaret's possession, Magda had started filing these documents when we were there in 1999-2000 and was still working on this same collection when I returned for a visit in 2005. It was to house this priceless collection that was the main reason for the restoration of St Edwards Chapel.

In 2005 the National Trust for Scotland started to advertise for new families to come and live in Canna, as they had failed miserably to stem the depopulation of the island.

When the NTS were gifted the island some 20 years earlier, there was more than 20 people there; by 2006, with Winnie's two girls now being educated in Mallaig, had it not been for the new primary school teacher bringing her two young children with her, the population of Canna would have dropped by 50 per cent.

Princess Anne unveiling the commemorative plaque at St Edwards Chapel

There was a huge response from people wanting to come, work and live on Canna.

Over 110 applied; families from Scotland, Germany, Australia and England, as well as a Polish family who were living in London. The initial 110 were reduced to 15 by the NTS then, with the assistance of the Canna people, the number was further reduced to six. These remaining six families were then invited to the island.

To me, deciding to live, bring up your family, and work on Canna, is not something that can be decided in one visit. It is being sold as being a beautiful, tranquil, idyllic island. Yes, on an afternoon visit in the middle of summer it may come over as being this, but there are two sides to every coin. Canna has been run by the same one family for over 40 years who are very set in their ways; you fall out with one member of the family and you find you have ultimately fallen out with everybody on the island. Everybody knows everyone else's business, and as we found, to our costs, some people stick their noses into your business for no other reason than to start malicious rumours. On a very small, isolated community, everybody ultimately relies on one another and you must work as a team.

Every team has to have a leader who must not abuse his or her powers, and must gain the respect of the full group otherwise it will simply not work. You cannot run away from problems and this is not made any easier when you also have to cope with a winter storm and the thought that the ferry might not turn up tomorrow.

CHAPTER SEVEN
# The final blame game

After all the excitement of the royal opening, we found ourselves being owed even more money. The architect, although promising, now refused to authorise the certificate for the additional decoration that was done to spruce up the Chapel, before Princess Anne's visit.

Lengthy negotiations took place over the next six months when the architect always reverted back to the problem of the water coming into the Chapel being caused by the high level pointing knowing fine that this was difficult to dispute, without re-scaffolding the building and inspecting the pointing up close. On release of some of the money owed to us, we agreed to re-erect the scaffold on the condition that if the high level pointing was faulty owing to poor workmanship, then we would pick up the re-scaffolding costs. However, if all the pointing works were found to have been carried out as instructed by the architect, then he would be liable for the costs.

This action was finally agreed on and we hired a landing craft from Kyle, capable of carrying 100 tonnes. Although our scaffold only weighed 20 tonnes, we required the deck space to also take out our tractor and trailer to transport the scaffolding from the pier, along the sandbar and up the new road to St Edwards Chapel. When the scaffolding was re-erected, another representative from the firm of architects came on site to inspect the pointing.

Every area that was selected as having a possible fault was found to have been completed as per architect's instructions. As you can imagine, these findings were not going down well with the architect himself. On our third such visit with the architect's representative, while he was frantically looking for faults in our work, he completely lost the place, and started to threaten and swear at me. It took me all my time to control myself but instead of retaliating, I calmly asked our workmen to gather up their tools, as it was not safe to be working under these conditions. We left the site and returned to Kyle.

I wrote to both the architect and the client as to why we had left the site, and informed them that we had tried our very best to resolve this long outstanding dispute, but without success. We heard nothing for the next two months. With the September gales fast approaching, for safety reasons we returned to site and removed the 340 scaffold boards and stored them on the ground. This left us with no other alternative than to use legal action to recover our money. On closer investigation, we found we still had not even been paid for the Canna road repairs, which were completed 15 months before.

It was only on receipt of this court letter that the client decided to bring in an independent mediator. We were informed that a company called Construction Dispute Resolution were to be employed by the Hebridean Trust to resolve this long-running disagreement. On receipt of this independent body being brought in we agreed to hold off the court recovery action. The first thing that Construction Recovery Solution wanted to do was to interview both the architect and ourselves. As we both had large files on this contract, it was decided that we should be interviewed separately in our own offices where, if required, we could access our files. On hearing this, the architect seemed to go into panic mode. Within days of hearing about the meeting, he dispatched a firm of steeplejacks to Canna by helicopter to carry out more spraying to the chapel walls.

Our first meeting with Construction Dispute Resolution took place in our offices in Kyle on the 15th of November 2001. This was to be the first of many meetings we would be asked to attend. Fortunately for us, we had kept a diary; every letter, fax, and the minutes of every meeting that had taken place during the contract. After attending a meeting at Glasgow Airport the architect informed us that he was walking away from all contractual responsibilities on St Edwards Chapel.

We were asked by the client to quote to re-erect the scaffolding around the bell tower of St Edwards Chapel. This tender was given on the clear understanding that 70 per cent of the costs would be paid within 14 days, with the remainder being paid when the scaffolding was dismantled because, we explained, we were sick fed up of being drip fed our money over the last year, only to find promises being broken and at the end of each visit finding we were owed even more money.

The scaffolding went up for the third time around the tower in April 2002, and as of 2006, that same scaffolding still remains round the tower. I was advised by the client that they had employed a specialist surveyor who would go out to Canna in February 2002 to make a further report on the water ingress. I was then informed that the weather was not suitable and the visit had to be delayed. "How," I asked myself, "was it acceptable to the client for this work to be delayed owing to bad weather when, two winters before, all hell broke loose if we were not working on the project because of adverse weather?"

We were also informed that a thermographic survey would be carried out on the chapel. Again we asked ourselves, why now, after the completion of the contract, all this research was being carried out on the chapel. Surely this survey work should have been carried out before the restoration works started. Or was it because a letter had turned up, a letter which had been written by the resident chapel priest, four years after the chapel was constructed, and sent to the original architect, complaining that the walls of the bell tower were leaking. The in-depth enquiry went on for 23 months and in this time we were asked to attend meetings in Glasgow, Fort William, Kyle, and on site on Canna. Before Construction Dispute Resolution were employed all three parties agreed to abide by their findings.

Construction Dispute Resolution found in our favour and recommended to the client that we should be paid for all the original contract works and also for all extra works we had been instructed to carry out. Much to our dismay, in October 2003 we were served with a further letter from a firm of solicitors in Edinburgh, informing us that they were now dealing with the disputed claim for St Edwards Chapel and that they were disputing our claim. We informed them of the enquiry's findings and that if necessary we were prepared to fight for our money in court.

It always amazes me that, although the client and his architect were prepared to use all the dirty tricks in the book to get their way, when you inform them that you are also prepared to hang out some dirty washing in a courtroom, that was not regarded as fair play.

To cut a long story short, a final settlement was reached in our office on the 15th of November 2003.

From then we heard nothing about St Edwards Chapel. We had given 15 months of our lives to this restoration work and were still very interested to find out what was happening to the building. We were informed that another £200,000 had been spent on re-pointing the outside of the building with two different contractors using lime pointing, but without further success. St Edwards Chapel was still leaking. We are the first to admit that the building trade of today has lost the lime skills it had 100 years ago. But why can architects of today not stand back and look at the problem from a different angle instead of wasting clients' money on an obsession that won't be successful.

Look at the facts: this building had been leaking from the date it was built. Why? Was it designed incorrectly for its location? Why was a bitumen based material painted on the inside of all the external walls, then these walls coated with a heavy tanking plaster? Because these walls were leaking and they were trying to contain the moisture within the walls in the hope of the moisture seeping down into the ground before penetrating through to the inside.

We could never understand why the architect instructed us to inject a damp proof course into the external stone walls round the entire building, preventing this seepage taking place.

Did he simply not understand the problem; had he not carried out enough research on the history of this building, or on the black-backed internal plaster sample they had taken in 1997? Lime pointing stone work on buildings in the centre of Edinburgh where these buildings are being protected by other buildings on all sides may well work, but it is simply not a suitable material to use to point a stone building (which does not have a built-in cavity) on a very exposed location, where the building is battered with gale-force winds and horizontal rain, for days on end, preventing the moisture from seeping back out. There are other materials now available within the building trade for this type of work.

In the summer of 2005 we returned to Canna to go and look at St Edwards Chapel. Annie my wife had also intended to travel with us. Fortunately she did not, because what we saw would have broken her heart. The back door was open, and going inside we found the building completely stripped bare — and I mean bare. Every item of furniture — bedding, video, TV, kitchen units, cooker, fridges, deep freezes, pots, pans, right down to the last item of cutlery — had gone. The building was filthy and we also found that all three toilets had been used but never flushed. When I think back to the day we left St Edwards Chapel in September 2000, when I went back to the chapel looking for Annie, only to find her on her hands and knees, scrubbing the linoleum floors, to leave them gleaming clean, only to now find the place so filthy that you could hardly recognise the patterned border on the lino floor. I am stuck for words to describe how disappointed I felt. Although St Edwards had now nothing to do with me I felt extremely angry that such a beautiful building would be treated with such disregard.

On that visit we noticed that the bridge between Canna and Sanday had been washed away and at high tide the residents of each island had to commute by rowing boat. Canna was alive with workmen building the new roll-on/roll-off ferry terminal, and much to my dismay they were using quarried rock material from the island. The road from the jetty to Canna House had also been repaired with the Type 1 road material that we had been prevented from using on the St Edwards Chapel road owing to its colour. This is a classic situation with the National Trust for Scotland: Don't do as we do, do as we say.

Government quangos such as SEPA and SNH and charities like NTS and the RSPB have a lot to answer for when it comes to looking after Scotland's wellbeing. The NTS were given Canna by the late John Lorne Campbell for its safe keeping and to preserve it for future generations. In my mind they are failing miserably to do this. They have not stopped Canna's depopulation. They destroyed the pedigree Highland cattle, which had been developed by the two previous owners by artificially inseminating this rare heard of highland cattle with continental semen, to try to increase their meat yield, thereby ruining 70 years of breeding.

The NTS also turn a blind eye when it suits them. They were happy enough to report us to SEPA (the Scottish Environmental Protection Agency) for burning rubbish on site when they quite happily watch all the Canna waste being tipped into a sea cove, where it is burnt and then twice a year, on a high spring tide, the remaining rubbish is dragged out to sea, only to finally wash up on all the other islands of the Inner and Outer Hebrides.

A very similar thing is happening on the neighbouring island of Rum, which was given to Scottish National Heritage on the condition that they would continue to run it as an open laboratory and continue the research work on the deer population that had been allowed to run free all over the island for the last 70 years, thereby developing into the most thoroughbred animals anywhere in the United Kingdom.

Only now to go against their word over the last few years SNH have been shooting the herd of deer, reducing their numbers to 1,200. They have now decided to plant trees on Rum. Trees that they do not intend to protect by fencing. For this to happen they intend to reduce the deer herd by a further two thirds, bringing the total number of deer on Rum down to 400, destroying seven generations of blood stock.

Quite how SNH think these remaining 400 animals will not eat the tops of the newly planted trees when they get hungry, I do not know. Maybe they will treat the deer like they treat the Scottish people. Give them a firm talking-to and inform them that they have been given government legislation to carry out this stupid planting programme. I think not — the deer will not be daft enough to listen to SNH! This may come as a great surprise to SNH who are used to getting their own way, irrespective of the devastating decisions they make. But sadly for the deer if they do not comply with the SNH legislation, they will probably be shot. A power, as yet, the present government has not given to SNH when it comes to dealing with the Scottish people.

When SNH were challenged about their decision, they said that the deer numbers had to be reduced to protect the trees. When asked why they were not fencing and protecting the young trees, their reply was that fencing would prevent people from walking on Rum. Have they never heard of gates or styles?

Sadly these duplicate government quangos are the ruination of our country. You only have to look at other islands in the Outer Hebrides to see the further devastation they are causing. In Lewis quangos are now objecting to the largest windmill development in Europe, which would offer the people of Lewis very skilful jobs, something which might hold these young people on the island instead of clearing away to the south looking for employment.

By objecting to these developments the quangos justify their existence, but it is you and I who pick up the bill. We are left with their huge legal costs; we also ultimately have to pay the bill for the local authority that are funding the public enquiry. We also, through time, pay the costs of the power company by our ever-increasing electricity charges.

The world is fast running out of carbon fuels and we urgently require to find alternative fuel sources. Scotland is surrounded by wind and wave power; let's welcome in this new technology to harness this source of power and stop sticking every conceivable obstacle in the way of those who are prepared to capture it.

How hypocritical of SNH. When you leave Inverness for the west of Scotland you are nearly blinded by the Dunain hillside lights all of which illuminate the SNH offices.

We have a saying in Scotland: Whoever pays the piper, picks the tune. If we don't put our collective foot down and stop pandering to every objection from these duplicate, government quangos, we will not have a country worth living in.

I will go so far as to say these quangos all have the same ultimate aim — to clear Scotland of its entire people. They are the second wave of Highland Clearances, only this time it is being fully funded by our Government.

We lost a golden opportunity to get rid of SNH when they refused to move to their new headquarters in Inverness. Instead of pandering to them and offering various financial incentives, we should have called their bluff and given them their redundancy. This would have been money well spent in the long run.